Introduction

Do we want a Planet we can live on in 20 years time?

If the answer is **yes**, then we may have to change the way we live our life, we will have to adopt values that will allow this to happen. Maybe you already have. We need to change our habits – all of us.

The human population has reached the stage where we need to understand that the Earth can only meet all our needs (let alone supply our wants) if we are careful and resourceful with the current resources. We need to apply permaculture principles to everything we do and consume.

Why?

Sadly it seems that this planet is dying. Anyone who takes the time to look and research can see that. It is not just that most of the fish stocks in almost all the seas around the world are collapsing; it is not just that most of the rivers are becoming polluted; it is not just that the atmosphere is changing, becoming more full of carbon dioxide, less oxygenated; it is not just that the ice caps are melting; it is not just that the sea levels are rising; it is not just that the climate is changing; it is not just that the soil is being eroded; it is not just that nuclear material is growing in quantity; it is not just that more and more toxic chemicals are produced every day; it is not just that there are more and more humans and less and less places for us to live; it is not just that the very air that we breathe is becoming more polluted with sulphur, with nitrates, with radioactivity, with carbon monoxide; it is not just that more and more of us are having poorer and poorer health; it is not just that crime appears to be on the increase; it is not just that the food we eat is less and less nutritious; it is not just that we are changing the very planet we stand and live on: it is the fact that it is all of these things together.

How is the Planet supposed to cope? How can we?

It is a fact that each of us leaves a "footprint" on this Planet, whatever we do, whatever we consume, it has an effect on everything else. We do not exist in isolation. An easy to understand example of this is the problem of climate change: if one country does nothing to decrease its output of carbon dioxide, then the whole world is still affected by the resulting increase in carbon dioxide in our atmosphere. However if no countries change to decrease their output of CO2, then the amount of CO2 can only continue to rise to dangerous levels.

How can we change this?

Simply follow the guidelines in this book, that's how. It is not a dogma, it allows for individual interpretation, you still have the freedom to be yourself but you will not be assisting in the devastating change of the planet. Both science and religion agree that the planet can be saved only with a change in human consciousness. That change has to start with each one of us.

We need to stop living in fear of what others may think of us. Do not continue to work in a job if you feel it is negative in some way. Feel the fear and do it anyway. You were born at this moment in time to help shape our Earth for its future. At the brink of environmental destruction we have the ability to save ourselves. We just need to stop talking about it and start doing it. In whatever capacity we can.

The simplest and easiest solution is to **stop consuming**. I found this the most liberating of all! I stopped buying anything that I did not need. No one needs a TV or the advertising that it supplies. Music is an art form and allows the expression of the Higher Self. It is uplifting and spiritual - yet it can also be destructive and dark. It is easy to listen to music that enhances the negative emotions. When I was in a bad state of mind, listening to gangster rap or heavy metal helped me feel that it is normal to feel this way - that it is OK to want destruction, to kill, rape, steal or consume. What are our children listening to? Is it good or right that 9 and 11 year olds are also listening to this?

Somehow we all have to find the strength to overcome our negative emotions and look deep into our heart to find our Spiritual Self. It is there. If you are alive, then you have a soul - whether you believe in its existence or not. I know many of us have had terrible upbringings. Parents who do not care - or worse, abuse either mentally or physically. The only person who can stop the hurt is yourself. It does not stop by passing it on. It stops by accepting it. I know it will take time - possibly 10, 20 years or more - in the meantime abuse of others or ourselves will not help and will only add to our misery. It is feeling sorry for ourselves and does not help. It does not stop the hurt. Acceptance is the only thing that does. This is the same for all of us. Buying new shoes, clothes, cars, videos, whatever does not fill the emptiness inside. We know this in our hearts - yet we still do it.

Those who do not have the money to consume in this fashion still want to do it. Yet it is pointless. Many of us take drugs in order to stop the emptiness inside. It works only while the drugs last and then we need more drugs to fill the space and then we have to say to ourselves that we are having fun. We convince ourselves that this is what life is about. Yet deep inside we know it is not true. We must accept ourselves for the people we are - even if we feel that our parents, friends or partner do not. It does not matter what others think. What matters is what we think of ourselves. If we do not like ourselves, we need to work out why and do something about it.

I have been through many of these phases and the only true answer I have found is meditation. Communing with my Higher Self - even if you think it is boring and there is no answer. We do exist. Ask yourself to come through to you. It is subtle. Rarely are there big lights and trumpet calls. Like the first time we smoke marijuana and do not think we are high... the first few attempts may be disappointing. Discouraging, even. But science has proved that Buddhists are happy. In our brains, there is a centre of happiness, the temporal lobe - true happiness and fulfilment and it is highly active in those who meditate on a regular basis. This then is true happiness, true freedom. This is the path to true happiness. Isn't that what we all want?

I have travelled to many countries and lived as part of many different cultures. I can honestly say that people in the so-called Developing World, those who have nothing - in the material sense of the word - are happiest. They may sit on the streets all day - yet they have the biggest smiles I have seen. Contrast that to the Western world where, in general, people have everything - or at least access to everything - and they are so miserable. Few walk around with a smile on their face and if they do, they are despised by the miserable ones.

I have noticed many westerners complaining about everyone and everything, they are unhappy and miserable. Of course this is a mass generalisation and I do know many happy individuals, but they seem to be the exception and not the rule. The very rich, the very powerful and the very famous are often the most miserable of all, or so we are led to believe from the media. Isn't it time we woke up to ourselves and started to see things from a different perspective?

How much longer are we going to stick our heads in the sand?

We do not even exist on this physical plane half of the time. Like the old 60 Hz cathode ray tube TV screen, each of us flickers on and off; in and out of this reality. Where do we go in the "off" phases? I often wonder. Our physical bodies are not the solid objects we like to think they are. This is not Eastern philosophy, this is Western physics. The 18th century physicist Boer, had a theory that every movement the body made was in fact the creation and dissolution of the physical form. Yet in both Eastern philosophy and Western physics they are saying the same thing: We are wavelets, wavelets, wavelets - mere passing of energy. To see, feel and experience the truth of this, we need to meditate. Not just once for a couple of minutes - but seriously. Work hard at it and we can experience this truth for ourselves. This is why Buddhists are happy. They understand the impermanence of everything and their place in the impermanence. Nothing stays the same. Everything changes. Some changes are faster than the human body can comprehend, some changes are far slower than the human body can comprehend. But believe me - it's all just ever-changing patterns of energy. Our purpose is to evolve spiritually until we can realize this on an experiential level. Only then will we be able to live in peace and harmony with other beings.

You will notice that I do not place small numbers with which to reference this work. Instead you will find a bibliography at the back and you are welcome to check out and do your own research. The reason for this is that I don't want you to take my word for it; find out the Truth for yourself. Go to a good search engine and check it out. Chlorine in water? Put it in, you'll find loads of info coming up. Please be aware that not everything you read on the internet is true, just like everything in the newspapers or on TV.

1. "Scientific facts" can uphold almost any theory you care to name. Much research is done to prove a particular theory and often evidence to the contrary is denied or ignored.
2. Nietsche said there were no facts, only interpretations and perceptions. The truth of this is obvious once you consider time to be a factor. 400 years ago it was a fact that the Sun moved around the Earth, it was only in 1936 that the Catholic church finally accepted that the Earth moves around the Sun. 500 years ago no

one had heard of germs and if you had said that there were invisible organisms that caused diseases, you would have been thought to be insane and possibly locked away. It wasn't until 1590s that microscopes were invented so these germs could be seen. So, facts change over time as we learn more about the world and find machines able to interpret it. Interestingly it seems we are now becoming so dependant on these machines that we take their readings as more valid than our own experience. In 2008, in the UK, a man drove into a river because his satnav told him it was a road! He believed what his screen told him, over and above what his own senses told him. Or maybe he thought his car could swim?

This is purely my interpretation, my perception of the "facts" as I see them. Others are welcome to deny this entire book and I fully expect many will – I write it because I want to increase your health and therefore the planet's health. Individually we cannot stop the world governments spending so much on weapons, when they could spend it on people. What we can do is look after ourselves and our friends in the most eco-friendly way possible. The more people that do this, the more likely it is that the world will come to its senses and stop producing these weapons. We will no longer need them as we will not live in fear anymore.

And so?

What is a Rainbow Warrior?

A Rainbow Warrior is one who has the belief that we need to be looking after our Earth much better than we are currently doing. Ultimately this is a selfish thing to do, for the human body evolved on a planet with very different compounds on it, so if we wish it to flourish we need to return the planet to a more similar state. We could literally be fighting for our children's and grandchildren's lives, for their right to grow up on a planet where they can breathe the air freely, drink from streams, springs and house taps without fear of poisoning, grow enough food to feed themselves without starving others.

A Rainbow Warrior would do what they can to protect the planet and thereby protect themselves and their future offspring. They can understand the importance of living for the future, rather than living in the past.

A Rainbow Warrior wants to look after themselves and their planet and will encourage all others to do so too.

The Warrior is balancing their chakras. There are many ways to do this: one needs to access each chakra in turn, meditate with each chakra, get to know it. Look at the areas of your life it refers to, what can be done to improve this area of your life? Working through each in turn, doing as much as you feel able to do at this moment, the warriors will bring about their own excellent health, be happy and live the life they should be living.

Who are the Rainbow Warriors?

The Warriors of the Rainbow are here right now, incarnated to show the Way. Maybe you are one and have forgotten? Maybe you are hiding? Our Earth needs every one of us right now. I believe that every one of us can be a Rainbow Warrior, you need only want to be one. Are you part of the problem or part of the solution? Just ask yourself these four questions and if the answers are positive, then you are a Warrior of the Rainbow!

Do you like animals or hate animals?

Do you like rainbows or hate the rainbow?

Do you like trees or hate trees?

Do you like people or hate people?

If you are still not sure, please read the prophecy in the appendix and if it moves you, then you are!

Environment and Health

The root chakra is red in colour and supplies us with raw energy. It is our instincts. It is what keeps us connected to our Earth. It is what keeps us grounded. Its watchword is "I trust the Universe"

The Rainbow Warrior needs to attend to each chakra in turn. The important thing is to aim to this, if you do not always succeed that is OK, keep trying. It does not matter which order you follow, just keep working your way through.

Environment and Health is at the root of the solution to our planet's problems, so this is the domain of the root chakra.

It's funny, you know? I thought this would be the easiest chapter for me to write yet it was the last chapter I attempted. I think it's because it's so big and covers the entire world! It's easy to feel overwhelmed by the enormity of it all. So I want to bring it back into perspective to make us realise that we do have control over our environment. **You can make a difference. Together we all make a big difference.**

I think the biggest problem I face, as an environmental activist is apathy. How can I bring out the caring and love that I am sure is in everyone, if only we would allow ourselves to feel it. How can I enable us all to see and feel that it is a part of our life too?

> We all live on this planet therefore it is up to all of us to look after it.

> There is much we can do to help in our own lives without changing them very much.

> All it takes is a change in perspective, you are obviously ready for that change otherwise you would not be reading this book!

Consumerism

One of the easiest, simplest yet most effective things we can do is change the way we shop. At least what we buy and where we buy it when we go shopping. I rarely buy anything that I do not need. There are times when want and need can be very subjective: do I want or need a MP3 player? I may decide that I want one but I don't need more than one. Or I may decide that I need an MP3 so I won't have a DVD player. Buy consciously rather than unconsciously, that's all.

Here are some ideas for conscious choices:

Buy local. Very simple, but very effective. It will, in the end save masses of carbon dioxide being produced. Today in Australia, we can buy spring water from Italy! Why? I am sure that Australia has its own very tasty spring water so why not buy that? Think of how many 1000s of air miles that water has travelled. Incredible! Incredibly stupid, more like. It is taking global capitalism to a ridiculous extreme. It is "world shopping" gone mad, for the sake of it and don't worry about the planet. Almost no one denies the existence of human-made climate change, with the notable exception of the current (No, this will not date, as whoever the population of USA vote for, the required president will get in,) US president and the company who bought him into power, Exxon-Mobil. Much can be done to reduce human impact on this planet without going back to the caveman days. Start reading the labels on food. Organic carrots from Israel! Why? Start questioning. Supermarkets are listening ever more closely to their customers, ever since the great E-numbers scandal, UK supermarkets have paid attention to and acted upon what their customers say. (Though not necessarily to the customer's best interests) Currently 70% of the UK's organic produce is imported. This is a rapidly expanding niche market. Buy from the local farm shop or good independent health food shop instead of the supermarket giants where possible. The food is fresher and tastes much better. It is also more likely to have less packaging. There are many organic box delivery schemes operating these days. Check them out!

Buy organic. We need to at least try to reduce the amount of processed food we buy. If we cannot pronounce what we read on the label: don't buy it! This is very relevant to shampoos, detergents and the like, but can still apply to food too. The E-numbers have been replaced by the full name of the chemical instead, so we still eat the same chemicals, we now know it is called erythrosine instead of E127. Erythrosine is a synthetic coal tar food dye, cherry red in colour. *Do we need something to be red that much?* Even in the studies I have read they say that more experimentation needs to be done to fully assess the effects on humans; yet we eat it in many foods already! We have done for decades. Could this chemical be another reason for decreased sperm counts in males? Or is it due to one of the thousands of other chemicals which have crept into our food. This effect was noted in mice back in the '60s, but our friendly governmental bodies said it was OK. So don't buy food that is processed. No one knows how good or bad it is for us.

Buy Fairtrade Products: When it is not possible to buy local, eg tea, coffee, chocolate, rice, sugar etc, please buy Fairtrade products. This makes a huge difference to the real lives of real people. There are those families who survive quite well because they produce for Fairtrade companies, unlike their neighbours who grow for normal traders and are literally starving. This is true all over the world, but I recently saw the case for it in Nicaragua. Spending an extra 40p here means a family in Nicaragua has enough to eat for the week. Think about that next time you buy some tea.

Be aware: refined white sugars and flours are addictive, so are fatty foods, especially the trans-fatty foods (e.g margarines and the like). The more we eat of them, the more we want to eat and are compelled to eat! It is just as poor for our health to be addicted to refined white sugar and flour, as it is to be addicted to heroin. It is also just as hard to come off. Don't believe me? Try going without any white sugar and flour for a week, and see how easy or otherwise it is. There is a "cold turkey" stage and the craving for doughnuts can be all but irresistible. At least that's how it felt to me. I confess to not having undergone a heroin cold turkey, but I think you can see my point. Do we want to condemn ourselves and our children to type II diabetes, various cancers and gouts, kidney failure and a host of other dis-eases, all due in part to chemicals in the poor quality food? Who is it that tells us that both meat and dairy products are vital for the body's well being and healthy growing up? Umm, gosh; it's the Meat and Dairy Marketing Boards. Hmm, doesn't sound entirely unprejudiced to me. I have been a healthy person without meat since 1985 and without dairy products since 2000. I really noticed a big change in my health after giving up dairy products. Try it, you might find you do too. Check out vegan websites for sensible dietary advice on doing this.

Ween our children off sugars and additives. Very difficult. They are not in our presence 24 hours a day. They may be fed orange squash at playgroup, swap lunches and sweets with their mates at school; all we can do is instil in them a sense of their own responsibility for their health and hope they agree. Don't forget to do this for yourself too. You may be amazed at what skin complaints disappear, allergies go, health returns. Fresh fruit is a delicious snack anytime of day, as are nuts and seeds. Use them as often as you like.

Honey, maple syrup and even raw sugar are better forms for the body than the refined white sugar which is used in processed foods.

So what else apart from food do we buy on a regular basis? Clothes? Make-up? Soaps and deodorants? Toilet tissue. Household cleaning products.

Let's start with toilet tissue.

Is there any reason not to buy recycled? After all, we are just using it once then throwing it into the sewage system. Also, please buy uncoloured, unbleached paper. The coloured paper has dyes in it that are not good for water life. (Think of the number of people in our country using this stuff every day! It's a heinous crime that they chop down 800 year old trees in Canadian temperate forests to make the non-recycled stuff!) Chlorine is the most toxic element on our planet (that isn't radioactive) and this is what is generally used to bleach all paper, including toilet paper. Though look out for the TCF or Totally Chlorine Free bleached products.

It's true that the process of recycling has its share of toxic products, but it's got to be better than chopping down 800 year old trees to wipe our bums with! Or am I wrong here? Of course, paper can be made out of many plants, not just trees.

Household cleaning products – including washing powders and washing-up. liquid:

Buy the eco-friendly products. Back in the 1950s, especially in the US, detergent companies became obsessed with ensuring that mothers and housewives became obsessed with cleanliness, whiter-than-white and sterility. Through TV ads they ensured that no house-proud woman would be without her Persil or Daz. The funniest thing is that it is only 2 companies that make almost the entire range of household cleaners we see in the supermarket today. Inside all of those different coloured boxes is the same white powder with blue flecks. These products which would have us believe that they are saving our lives from drudgery, are in fact destroying all the watercourses around us. I am sorry to say that many of them lie about the "greenness" of their product. "Low phosphate" they tell us, in comparison with high phosphate ones perhaps, but multiply that by the number of people who use the stuff and the many who overdose their machines and there is still enough phosphate being washed into our waterways to feed several acres of algal blooms every day. They are also in the main oil-derived. Not something we'd immediately consider as being what we'd want to wash our clothes in, or wipe down our surfaces with.

These days there are plenty of green alternatives. They are vegetable-based and will always be labelled as such. They contain no phosphates or enzymes and will usually say so on the label. The enzymes found in biological powders can interfere with the natural processes of aquatic life, so are just as bad as phosphates and chlorine for water life. Many of our cleaning products are deadly to other life forms (and even ourselves!).

 Do not overdose. The number of house-shares I have been part of, I know that huge numbers of people seem to think that if they just pour in more liquid or powder, they won't actually have to do any washing! Use some elbow grease instead along with a scrubby sponge or brush. A 250ml bottle of washing up liquid should last over 2 months. We only need a few drops of the stuff. I have been in flats where people go through it in under a week! What are they doing? Not using any water in the sink? Similar with washing powder. If our clothes are badly stained, we can use one of those anti-stain things instead of 3 times more powder than usual. It will save us money and save the watercourses. Read the label. Follow the instructions on dosing.

What about those we use on ourselves? I would advise reading the labels on our shampoos, soaps and deodorants. Most of these products are oil-based. Be careful of claims of "natural" and "organic" as in this case, they are often referring to a very small percentage of the product as being of natural origin. As for the organic; those who are chemists amongst us will recognise this term to mean organic chemistry, i.e. anything with a few carbon atoms strung together. This is also the meaning mostly used by the same companies that bring us our washing powders and detergents! Hmm. Sounds like we are washing ourselves with petroleum products. Especially check out Body Shop products, which are rife in these compounds, yet the marketing of these would have you believe that they are lovely, natural and organic. However the truth is that they are only "Not tested on animals" because they use compounds that were tested on animals 20 or 30 years ago and therefore are now considered safe, so do not need to be tested further.

Labels
So what should we look out for?

1. Petro-chemicals are often prefixed by **methyl-**, **ethyl-**, **butyl-**, **propyl-**. This refers to the number of carbon atoms in the longest sequence. They are often suffixed by **acetate** or **paraben**. These are oil-derivatives and are toxins to our bodies. We wouldn't eat oil, so why should we pour it all over our skin?

2. I would also avoid **benzo-**, **pheno-**, **phospho-**, **benzyl-**, **phenyl-**, prefixes. These are known carcinogens. Very toxic to the human system.

3. Look out for chemicals with names so long that they just write in the letters, such as **PEGs**, **EDTA**, **DEA**, which appear in many shower gels. These are also oil-derived and often carcinogenic.

4. Anything ending in **–ol** is an alcohol and may result in the product being labelled as organic (As in organic chemistry, as described earlier), so would anything ending in **–one** (an ester) and **–amine** contains nitrogen and is also part of the organic chemistry compounds. Some alcohols are less drying than others, so check it out for yourself. See below for how.

5. If a chemical has **chloro-** anywhere in its name, it contains the chloride ion, if it has **diazo-** it is double nitrogen, **thia-** means sulphur is present. If in doubt, write down the chemical and go to www.google.com or a similar search engine, type in the name and see what comes up.

Also just because a chemical was derived from a natural product, doesn't mean that it is always good for you, or natural anymore. There are many foaming agents derived from coconut, but the processes the coconut has gone through to extract these chemicals means that the product is far from natural. Also once removed from its whole and used in isolation, this changes the properties of the compound. Eg. aspirin is not at all like willow bark, yet the compound for aspirin was originally found in willow bark, but it would be wrong to say that an aspirin is a natural product. However if cosmetic companies were marketing it, they would claim it was a natural product, just like the labels on many shampoos and shower gels do.

As I said before, many labels lie. In many countries there are very poor labelling laws and products can say almost what they like without having to substantiate their claims. There are some ridiculous labels these days, such as "gluten-free" on crisps (potatoes have never had gluten in them), or "sugar-free" water! Amazing, what will they think of next? Some companies are marketing themselves in a very bizarre manner, such as Nestle, in Spain calls itself "the nutrition expert", which is very odd considering how much confectionary it produces and how few nutritional products you will find made by them.

"I don't have time to read all the labels on everything I buy!" we cry. The point is we would not have to read everything all the time. It only takes one reading to see what is in it and we can remember not to buy it next time. Do some research on it for yourself. (Because I am afraid we should not trust the government agencies to do appropriate testing, as they do not, or are subject to financial inducements which some might call bribes, as was proved with the GE debate.) We can take a picture with our smartphone of the label in a shop and look it up, either at the time, or at home later. It need only take a couple of glances on the internet and we'll have plenty of information to be going on with.

Many health food shops sell good, non-chemical ranges of soaps and shampoos but still check the labels. Again, the basic guide is; if it's in English (as opposed to Latin plant names) and we still have difficulty pronouncing it – don't buy it!

Many of us are probably thinking "if these chemicals are so dangerous, why are they in our shampoos? Why aren't they tested?" I found out during my university studies for pharmacology that they are tested on animals for skin-reactions. They are not tested for long-term use. No one is shampooing rabbits' fur for decades to see if it starts to fall out! (If only because rabbits don't live that long, especially the ones in testing laboratories!) Does the rabbit's eye swell? That is what is being tested. The rabbit may be dissected afterwards, but no one is checking its lymph system for weird chemicals or disfigured lymph nodes – assuming it is even wise to extrapolate such results to humans anyway! Most of these oil-based products are being tested long-term on humans now. For the past 70 years we have subjected ourselves unknowingly to these tests and the results may be coming back in the form of increased rates of asthma, allergies etc. in the young. None of this can be scientifically proven, as there is no "control" group. There is no scientific evidence of what is causing all these allergies and vastly increased rates of asthma. There is no scientifically managed experiment happening: yet we are subjected to a whole host of technological breakthroughs for which there are no tests, no proofs, no way of telling if any one dis-ease is caused by any one of the 1000s of new chemicals released every year into our environment. No one is testing what happens when some of these chemicals meet. If we remember our science classes at school, we might remember that chemicals form bonds with each other. Chemical reactions occurred in our test tubes and we had to write the result down. Chemical reactions don't just occur in test tubes. They are happening right now in our environment. What reactions occur, what new chemicals are being made? There is no way to tell. You would think we would have more sense and stop producing yet more; but we don't. Gotta keep those profits coming in, guys.

On top of that we continue to add more dangerous toxins to our global environment, such as radioactive waste and there is a plethora of unknown possible problems with the release of genetically altered plants growing in 10,000s of acres across the US, Canada, Australia, Asia; wherever the biotech companies can force their hand with that spoonful of honey called money.

What's wrong with buying clothes? It depends on where they were made. A small, local firm whose factory we pass by every day on our way to work: nothing. However, once we start buying from the big High Street names, we should question the origin. Does the label say "Made in Britain"? or "Made in Taiwan"? I know that in some Third World sweatshops the workers are doing gruelling 14 hour shifts for £5 a week, children sleeping in dorm rooms, torn away from their families when they are as young as 10 years old. They sew "Made in Britain" labels onto the clothes they make. This is true of anything from our head to our feet. And yet, these children are lucky; they have not been sold into sex slavery. They have not been brutally and repeatedly raped until they have no spirit left. They have not been tortured so rich, white, impotent, Western businessmen who cannot force their ways on Western women can do what they wish to these poor girls and boys.

It is truly a sick world we live in, but each one of us can make a difference. Buy second-hand clothes. Buy from smaller companies. Be daring – make our own clothes.

The more of us that turn away from the Transnational Corporations the more of us will be supporting small, local producers. We will be creating positive alternatives. We need to get the planet back on an even keel, especially if we are to keep increasing our numbers. It is the greed for ever-increasing profits that is causing the destruction of our planet. Yet it doesn't have to be that way. Join a LETS scheme, Local Energy Transfer System. Instead of using money to pay for all the goods and services we need, we rack up credits and debits instead. In any LETS there will be a group of people with particular skills to offer; this could be anything from child-minding, to accounting, teaching the internet, massages, carpentry, self-grown food, plumbing, quite literally anything. Then we trade services via the credits with other people in our group. You paint a picture for someone and charge them 50 LETS credits, in turn you use 30 LETS credits for a massage for yourself. And so it goes.

These trading schemes exist in the big cities as well as smaller towns and it's a great way to meet new people! We might even find someone to make fantastic "own design" clothes for us.

This world is about doing what we want but it can no longer be at the expense of others.

Buying make-up. Once again the manufacturers suggest we cover our skin – the body's largest organ, which we are supposed to breathe through – with a range of oil-based chemicals that have been tested on animals to see if they cause a rash.

Many women are cajoled into this form of torture. Stop doing it! I know for many women it is considered as part of their uniform, but do we really need to have a job that asks us to destroy our skin? There must be something else we'd rather do. Or if not, we could spend that extra money on non-oil-based products and allow our skin to breathe.

There are so many books on the small things we can do to save the environment, get them out of the library and read them and actually do what they suggest.

The only way to escape this, to restore ourselves back to living in harmony with the planet, instead of arrogantly insisting we know better than the grand design, is to change the way we think. We have to stop this utter madness of "capitalism at all costs" and understand that it is possible to have "economic growth" without stripping our Earth bare of all her resources. It is possible to make a profit whilst putting people and the planet first. Not only possible, but also desirable and even economically the best solution!

Our very existence in the long-term requires that we do this. If we are to

continue to live on this planet, we have to start employing this ideology now!
If we do not, the consequences for all life on this planet are dire **and that
includes me, you, our family and our friends.**

How can we make this turn around? We can start with our own life. In fact
that is all that we can do. We cannot make anyone else change, but we can
change ourselves. We can make that extra bit of effort to buy local, organic
produce. To start growing a few carrots and onions in our back gardens. To
think about what toxic chemicals we are pouring down our drains and stop
doing it. There are less toxic alternatives. Use them! I know many will say
that the green washing powder doesn't get the white clothes, whiter-than-
white. No. It won't. It doesn't contain the optical isomers that focus UV light
onto the fabric. *But isn't safeguarding our planet worth that?* If we can
change our view of clean to mean "free from dirt" instead of "whiter-than-
white"; then maybe we will have a planet for our grandchildren to grow up
safely in, one where they don't have to buy clean air tanks so they can
breathe properly.

One thing is for sure: do nothing and we are ensuring that mutually assured
destruction will come upon us anyway. We, like the Romans and other great
empires, will slowly lose our power, our grip on the physical world. Dying
younger and younger from asthma, cancers, diabetes, AIDS; any number of
dis-eases because we are failing to honour ourselves, failing to honour what
tribal natives call "The Great Spirit" and failing to honour our home, this
planet Earth.

We are at the crossroads now. This coming decade will spell our end. Are we
going to let corporate greed run our life for us, or are we going to take back
our life? The choice is ours. Be part of the solution, not the problem. Doing
nothing is also the problem.

What a Load of Rubbish!

A huge difference we can all make is to stop producing so much rubbish!
World over we are running out of landfill space, we are passing our rubbish
onto other towns and countries to deal with, because there is too much for us
to deal with ourselves! How ridiculous! There should be a tax on the amount
of rubbish each household produces, a tax for businesses too. Walking down

the road I see many shops placing their cardboard outside to go in the dustcarts, yet there are cardboard recycling schemes all over. Why? Can't be bothered. That's all. It seems like we cannot be bothered to save ourselves, it's too much effort! In nature nothing is wasted. It's time we took a leaf out of nature's book, after all she's been around a lot longer than we have. Everything in nature is recycled, as the old saying goes "one person's trash is another person's treasure". Time to start living by this motto again. More simple points to consider:

1. **Simple things like don't buy over-packaged products**, don't buy that product. Change our habits. If we have to buy our organic food from a supermarket, we soon find ourselves in a quandry over whether to buy "normal" produce because then we don't need to buy all the packaging that is on the organic produce! Buy organic produce from the farmer's markets or our local health food shop. Not buying plastic bottles seems almost impossible these days as so many drinks come in them: so don't buy these drinks. Stick to juices, which tend to come in cartons, or concentrates which are often in glass rather than plastic. Many carbonated drinks are packaged in plastic, so don't buy them. They are not good for us anyway, we have already enough carbon dioxide in our systems without readily drinking it!

2. **Write to companies** and tell them that you will not buy their products because they are over-packaged. If they start to receive a few emails a week about their products, they'll soon change. Marketers will tell a company that if they receive one email about something, then there are 700 people feeling the same way. So our email represents 700 people, not just one! Imagine if only 1/10th of the people reading this book wrote to companies and told them this? This could result in the company thinking a bit more about its packaging policy and may well result in it reducing the amount of packaging, or changing from plastic, which is not easily recyclable, if at all, to glass, which is easily recyclable, or paper (recycled, of course!).

Plastics and cling films often leach undesirable chemicals into the very food they are supposed to be protecting! So as well as being toxic in their production, they introduce toxins into our food and drink. Especially fatty foods, so no more milk in those plastic bottles!

3. **Recycle all we can**. This includes our old furniture, computers,

TVs. There's always someone who needs what we don't need. Many towns have furniture recycling schemes and charity shops will always accept our old clothes and bric a brac. Check out the classified ads in the local paper. Someone will pay us money for our old stuff, or at least cart it away for us, to be used elsewhere. Your local Facebook group is an ideal place to sell unwanted items.

4. **Finally we have to throw something away**: make sure it is as small as possible before it goes into the bin. This means that there is less volume in the bin bag, thus saving us money as we don't go through so many bin bags. This also means less plastic going into landfill sites. Plastic is not biodegradable and will stay in the ground for thousands of years. Try to compost if possible. Ask the local council to create a composting scheme. If all our food waste went into making compost instead of landfill, our farmers would find it much easier to grow organically and our landfills wouldn't be full of methane gas. The waste could be used to fuel bio-gas systems to heat our houses with. There are many, many better ways to deal with our waste than what occurs currently. I even know of one scheme where food waste was collected regularly and given to pigs. Even better.

When so many councils run doorstep recycling schemes there really is little excuse not to do even this small thing. All we have to do is spend 30 seconds washing the container out and put it in our box and there we go. We have saved the planet in a small, but important way. If we don't have doorstep recycling, we can find our own box and make the effort to go out to the recycling bins on the street or at the local supermarket or to the local recycling centre. It's not that hard, once we make it a habit. 21 days is all it takes.

<u>Action Points</u>

- Buy local, organic, natural products where possible
- Buy Fairtrade where possible
- Check the labels of everything we buy at least once
- Do not buy polluting, oil-based products
- Choose Green alternatives for every product we buy
- Join a LETS scheme
- Think about the impact we have on the Planet and ensure that it is a small one
- Refuse, Reduce, Reuse, Recycle. In that order
- Squash all boxes, cans, plastic containers etc.
- Compost as much as we can
- Don't buy over-packaged goods
- Write emails to companies and councils; tell them our views
- Make our own clothes or buy second hand
- Cut down on our consumerism
- Buy recycled stuff wherever possible
- Do our own research on various chemicals we find on labels
- Recycle all our old stuff (take it to the charity shop)

Daily Exercise

The sacral chakra is orange in colour and represents a healthy yin-yang. It is about reproduction and emotions. There can be sexual violence when it is blocked. Use it to express your creativity, to dance and to have fun! The second chakra is vital for Warriors to have control of. We need to be fit and healthy for the fight for our planet.

Anger is one emotion that seems to cause the most damage for people on all levels. Physical exercise can be a fantastic way to release anger. It can be a great way to balance your second chakra.

We all know we need daily exercise, but how many of us actually do it? It seems so hard to fit into our daily lives. We don't have the time for it. We don't have the energy for it. Our work life has tired us out too much. It's all too much bother.

Yet daily exercise is vital for our well being and it needs to be on all levels. I am not just talking about physical exercise here – but also mental and spiritual exercises.

Physical

The physical exercise must be something we enjoy doing – otherwise we will not do it – it will become a chore for us. It needs to be something that we look forward to. Perhaps we can cycle to work, thereby feeding two birds with one scone; getting our physical exercise in and saving the planet. When I was able to cycle to work, it felt fantastic and I felt great. I was living in London at the time, but still managed to find a route through parks and down less-used side streets to arrive safely.

Swimming is usually an excellent option if we live by an unpolluted river or sea. If we are really lucky, our local pool may be ozone-bleached rather than chlorine-bleached.

Why is chlorine so bad? It is the most toxic element on our planet – it kills everything, even our atmosphere and ozone layer! Why the authorities see fit to put it in our drinking water and drown our swimming pools in it, I shall never understand. I know it kills bacteria etc but it should then be removed from our water supply. The taste is very strong, but it is available and cheap.

We breathe through our skin – it is a wonderful semi-permeable membrane, which keeps water out, yet also absorbs nutrients, small molecules and therefore is capable of absorption of toxic elements such as chlorine. Thus if our house's water supply is contaminated with chlorine, we had better think twice about those hot showers we currently enjoy. If we can see the steam from our shower – i.e. the bathroom mirror is fogged – we are absorbing chlorine through our skin as we wash. The same is true of a hot bath. There are filters available that can be put on the house water supply. Swimming pools – having a far greater concentration of chlorine than our average drinking water supply – are still great places to absorb chlorine even though the water temperature is low in comparison.

Although swimming is one of the best exercises for our muscles, it might be the most polluting thing for our body!?!?!

What can you do about it? Ask the local baths to switch to ozone. Tell our friends and swimming club members. Get people on our side and force a change of policy. Then we can return to the local pool and swim safely.

Ask the council or the water company if they will remove the chlorine from the water after treatment, instead of leaving it in the water supply that we drink. Buy a water filter for our tap water. You can get ones that go direct onto the mains supply before it comes out of the tap. If the tap is not yours, then buy a filter jug. More expensive in the long run, but it doesn't require any kind of plumbing. ;-) They say you can pour the water and leave it, the chlorine will evaporate from the water surface. Certainly a cheap option, though I do not know how effective it would be.

Push-ups (either against a wall or on the floor) are good, as are sit-ups. We need no special equipment, the weather does not matter, as long as we have space to lie down - they can be done. I recommend a series of 20 push-ups, followed by 10 sit-ups to start with for 3 or 4 rounds. We can then increase the number of each exercise by 10 until we feel we are really working our muscles.

Any exercise is good, as long as we enjoy it. That's the main thing.

When cycling always wear a cycle mask when in traffic. If we do not, we can do more damage to ourselves through the intoxication of carbon monoxide (CO) than any health benefits we might be gaining. Jogging may not as good for us as we are tempted to believe – it's bad for our knees and again, if we're close to traffic, we'll need a mask.

I am tempted to say go to a gym. Here there are people who are trained in body training, who can help us find the right exercise program. We are inside, so we don't breathe polluted air – but we don't get much fresh air either.

It's all a compromise – how to live safely in this toxic world – preferably without becoming so paranoid that we do nothing, or becoming so blasé that we don't care and accept it all.

Games of football, rugby or hockey with our mates are excellent ways to boost energy, get us out and about and socialising. It's the pints of beer in the pub after that's the problem – undoing all the good work our body has achieved in the previous hour and a half!

Tennis, squash, badminton – all excellent. Ice/roller-skating is very good for the body. As I said, it's the enjoyment that counts – this ensures we want to practice and that we make time to do so. If we do not enjoy our exercise it becomes easy for us to stop, or not bother, or lose rhythm. If it becomes a social thing or it is so much fun, we will want to do it no matter what.

<u>Mental</u>

As a practitioner of tai chi since October '92, I would obviously heartily recommend it to everyone. Truly it is a wonderful exercise; keeping us physically, mentally and spiritually fit. I have taught many people tai chi and qi gong – not a single person has told me they haven't gained benefit and only a very few have not returned to each class and completed the course.

Tai chi and qi gong teach the body to breathe properly, to relax, to stretch our body in an effective, yet gentle manner. They are both excellent exercises for improving balance, posture, circulation, oxygen absorption, stamina and endurance. They decrease fatigue and high blood pressure; because of their gentleness, they are the perfect exercise for those who are old or infirm – those too ill to exercise, yet who really need it. Tai chi and qi gong improve joint flexibility and stave off arthritis and natural joint degeneration. The slow and gentle movements can allow damaged joints and spine to heal and improve. As all the muscles and joints are gently exercised during the practice, muscle tone is improved and then strengthened, every muscle being contracted and relaxed. This includes the smooth muscles of the digestive tract, which are rarely exercised outside of digestion. Co-ordination and fine motor control are also improved, leading to an increased reactive system. As one must concentrate in order to learn the movements accurately, the attention is focused and in time we experience the meditation within the movement. Thus, it is the perfect exercise to de-stress both body and mind.

I am sure I could continue to fill this book with the benefits of tai chi – but I will not. There are plenty of books on the subject. Go read one and find out for yourself! This is not the way to learn the exercises however. We should only attempt to learn from a teacher. Go to a class. Practise tai chi and/or qi gong. Qi gong is a breathing exercise that is a standing form of tai chi. It uses many similar movements and has many of the same benefits. It has the added advantage of needing less space, which can be useful, if we live in a small flat, or have only a small garden to practice in.

If we cannot practice tai chi, then please try out yoga. Both exercises have similar effects; they just have different perspectives – one Chinese, one Indian. As I said to one person, if you do one – there is little point in learning the other. It is analogous to PCs and Macs. Both do the same job, have similar effects, but their operating systems are quite different and to chop and change between the two can be quite confusing. If we are learning one system – keep to it. There is no need to learn both. It may even make us less effective at the one we do know, to practice the other. We start to forget which buttons do what on each system.

The very least one can do is a daily exercise of chi building. It is very simple and if we start to find good results; maybe we will be enthused to find a tai chi, qi gong or yoga class.

How? Just stand naturally, feet shoulder width apart (check in a mirror), back straight – but relaxed. Hold our hands out in front of our abdomen (or tan tien) about 20 cm (8 inches) apart, palms facing each other. Slowly move the right (or left) hand in a slow circle opposite the other hand. Breathe quietly and naturally as we do so. Start to breathe down to the abdomen, in through the nose and out through the mouth. This is good practice for breathing. Many people breathe poorly.

After a while we can start to feel our own chi (personal energy that every living being has); perhaps as a pressure, or tingling sensation, maybe as heat or a combination of these: no matter, as we become more sensitive, we <u>will</u> feel something.

Continue for a few minutes – as long or as short as we like. When we have enough or are bored; throw our chi ball over our face, pour it down our body. If we have some pain or illness let our hands rest over the affected area for a short while.

Try to think of nothing – or at least make our thoughts pleasant ones; certainly not – 'ooh, better pay the phone bill today' or 'must remember to pick Johnny up from swimming lessons'!

<u>Sex</u>

The best, certainly most fun regular exercise I can think of is sex! Yes, that's right. Sex. It used to be taboo, then it wasn't and now it is again as everyone is so scared of STDs. However, with the right person (or persons ;-)) it is the most joyful pastime we can have.

The only rules I would have are "Cause no emotional hurt to anyone, including yourself" and "Do what is right for you". If it coincides with what is right for another… then bingo! Ya got it going on!

Not only is sex a lot of fun but it is one of the best tension releasers I know of. All the tai chi and yoga and whatnot is good, but I have to admit that some good lurvin' just reaches the parts that chi building can't reach. I love sex and don't function so well without it on a regular basis. I believe it is a natural and healthy part of being a human. There is nothing bad about it.

It is unfortunate that few people don't just do as they would like when it comes to this recreation. I believe the world would be a happier place if we did. So many of us get hung up on jealousy and other negative emotions surrounding this excellent exercise. Sex is a natural and normal part of most adult humans' lives. Let's face it, none of us would be here without it! Most humans need sex in order to be happy and truly healthy beings. If only we could admit that and not insist on trying to make it all so complicated, often to the extreme of making it seem unnatural.

Due to our need for sex, it often seems desirable to set ourselves up with a steady-sex partner. This usually turns into a "relationship" and this is sometimes where the problems begin. I believe we should all be free to make love as time and circumstances dictate. No one should feel any obligation to have sex; no one should feel restricted with the sex they can have. Both of these are possible, we must just be careful choosing our partner. Monogamy is not a natural state for many mammals and that includes humans. The mass failure of faithfulness in human sexual relationships surely demonstrates this. So why try to pretend it is? Why are we not honest about our own nature? Undoubtedly there are couples that are and remain entirely faithful to each other till death do they part. Good on them. That's really great and wonderful for those concerned. However, in this day and age it seems such couples are no longer the norm (if indeed, they ever were).

We all lead such busy lives, more work-oriented, less family oriented, so many meetings, hard to juggle a social life as well as school, college or university. It becomes very hard to plan our lives around others. Why do we feel the need to control our partner's life? Or be controlled by them? We suck energy from other people; we try to feel full by draining someone else. We wonder why our relationships fail after 3 months, 6 months, 3 years, 7 years? Once we feel our own power and feel strong enough in ourselves (connected with the Universe) then we can have partnerships with more than one person. Or even not. Just love many people very dearly. Not feel the need to live with them constantly, to refuse all others just to be with our "one love". The one should also be secure enough in themselves to know that we love them. They know we will always come to them.

I am not saying that it is impossible to be faithful, just that it is not a natural state for humans. There is some evidence for this if you look at the pace at which sperm swim. Gorillas live a monogamous lifestyle and accordingly their sperm swim quite slowly. Chimpanzees on the other hand are very promiscuous and their sperm swims much faster. Human sperm swims at a speed that's between the two. If we are in a monogamous relationship and loving it, then that's fantastic! Many people are not, however. We are beings of light and love, come down into this physical plane to love and play. What works for one being, does not necessarily work for another. So, throw off the shackles of religion or phobia or societal norms and be what we want to be. Love whom we want to love, as often as possible. It can be one person, or several people. It can be the same sex or opposite sex or both. We have the freedom to choose - so let's do it.

Do what makes you happy often.

There are many special things we can do with sex. This includes tantric meditation. It is possible to become so high during intercourse that our mind seems to enter another dimension and we experience something akin to astral projection or hallucinogenic drugs. This is not something to be scared of and is completely controllable. I will not go into details here, as there are many good books on the subject. If you do wish to know more – check out the bibliography in the back.

If we are not getting any sex with a partner, then have sex with our self. Spend time getting to know our own body, find out what we like. Pamper ourselves, give ourselves a great aromatherapy bath then massage our self all over with olive or coconut oil. Enjoy our self.

<u>Spiritual Exercise</u>

No exercise regime is complete without some form of meditation. Most people in fact meditate in one way or another – usually without realising it, or calling it meditation. Meditation is really just a way of tuning into our inner being. For most people in Western society (and increasingly in other cultures too), this is achieved through watching TV. The main problem with this form of meditation is that it is highly unfocussed and often fills our head with unnecessary extraneous thoughts, which rather goes against what meditation is really all about. Those who jog, cycle, run, swim or do any other form of "alone" sport often fall into meditative trance without realising it. It can even happen whilst we are driving our car or walking a well- known route. During a journey, have you ever suddenly realised you are further along than you thought and wondered how you got to 'this bit already'? Where did our mind and thoughts go? We cannot remember what we were thinking. Well, that was a meditative trance.

If we find this happening to ourselves on a regular basis, we should seriously consider practicing some form of formal meditation. Our soul is obviously crying out for it – even if we do not believe we have one and believe that this is the only life there is. Meditation is not against any form of religion, nor does practicing it make one a religious person. The two are irrelevant to each other. We do not have to give up any of our current beliefs in order to meditate; we do not have to start having new beliefs in order to meditate.

I often think how different the world would be if every single one of the nearly 8 billion who live here were to meditate for even 10 minutes a day.

Perhaps we feel that we as each individual are too small or too inferior to make a difference. Not so. Have you ever spent the night with a mosquito, midge or flea? Then you understand that no one is too small to make a difference.

If we wish to save the world, we have to save ourselves first. Until each of us have food and shelter, love and happiness, we will not have the time or thouht to save our planet. Food and shelter are relatively easy to find but love and happiness? These concepts are not so easy. We will not find them in the outside world – I have found that we need to start by loving and respecting ourselves. Once we have that we can begin the journey to true happiness.

True happiness does not come from material objects – as is easily evidenced by the lives of most of the rich and famous. It does not come from power over others – as is evidenced from any political leaders. True happiness comes from within.

I am not saying that having material objects will make us unhappy – just that the acquisition of them will not lead us to true peace and happiness. There are those who say that a perfect society is impossible – or that Utopia would be boring. I do not believe so. We can have dissent amongst humans without it turning to bloodshed or power sucking.

The main problems in the world are caused by uneven power distribution. Those who are "in control", I see as being insecure and weak. They feel they have to take power from others in order to build themselves up. This is simply not true.

If every human on the planet learned to meditate, we would each realise that we are all-powerful beings who can and do change the world to our liking. We could grasp our own power and not feel the need to steal it from others.

How do you meditate? There are many styles and forms of meditation – we simply try whatever suits us. It may take a while to find the right one.

One of the simplest is vipassana, ideally we need to go on a 10-day course to really get the feel of it, but there is no reason not to just simply start with anapana meditation. Anapana requires that we just sit quietly and concentrate on our breathing. That's it. Feel our breath coming in and out of our nostrils. Don't count it; don't control it. Just observe it. Even 10 minutes a day is better than not doing it at all. We will not feel the full benefits from just 10 minutes, but maybe we will start to want to do it for longer. Do this for ideally an hour in the morning and an hour in the evening. Maybe we will eventually decide to do a vipassana course and discover the benefits of vipassana for our self.

Rarely do we have time to ourselves. If we have children – try to persuade them to join us. This will start to give us the time we need.

There are many forms of meditation – chanting over again a mantra of some kind; focusing our attention on some kind of image – be it a statue, a photo, a flower, a flame; then there is tai chi; tantric sex; focusing on the chakras; imagining a column of light through the body, connecting our physical self to our Higher Self to the centre of the Earth and many more.

All of these are good – there is no bad meditation – they all have the same purpose:- The idea is to become still in mind, body and spirit: to start to come to terms with the real you. To realise that everything that exists within the universe – us included – is all just ever-changing patterns of energy. Ask a physicist, they will tell you this.

Why are we here? To evolve spiritually until we realise this on an experiential level, only then will we be able to live in peace and harmony with other beings. Is it really that simple? Yes! We all must start with ourselves if we are to experience true peace, true happiness in our current three-dimensional, space-time continuum.

An exercise that can solve most of our problems is this:

For five minutes, concentrate on the fact that the point of power is in the present. Feel and dwell upon the certainty that your emotional, spiritual and psychic abilities are focused through the flesh and direct all your attention on what you want. Use visualisation or verbal thought, whichever comes best to you, but focus only on your wants, not on your lacks. Use all of your energy and attention for these five minutes, then forget it. Do not check to see if it is working. Simply make sure that your intentions are clear. Then in some way, make a gesture that is in line with your belief or desire. e.g. If we want to be rich, act as if we are rich. Buy something that costs more than we would usually pay for it. If we are lonely and wanting friends, smile at someone. If we are ill, do something that we would do if well. Make sure these are small things and feel certain that our belief will ensure we come to no harm through these actions. This will only work if we cease to look for "what is wrong".

We must stop reinforcing negative beliefs. This is true for everything.

<u>Sleep</u>
It might seem strange that I include a section on sleep in the chapter on
exercise, but without sleep we could not function. Another source of great
unhappiness is poor sleep. Think about how cranky we feel if we do not have
our usual amount of sleep, whether that is 5, 8 or 10 hours per night.
Scientists have done much research on sleep and concluded that it is vital for
our well-being. We crave it if we do not get it and it is a well-known form of
torture to deprive a person of sleep. I think the most a person has gone
without sleep is 73 hours. Manchester University also tried some sleep
deprivation experiments on a couple of raw foodists. They managed 120
hours without sleep and were performing well in various tasks set by the
scientists. Yet for most of us we cannot do without it. It is possible that
without it we would die, yet scientists have been equally baffled by why we
actually need it. What is it for? Yes, the body needs rest, as does the brain. It
has been proven that different parts of the brain are active during sleep than
are active when we are conscious. It has also been proven that there are
different parts of the sleep time. There is the well-known REM sleep, during
which we dream and the other phase of sleep, which is much longer in
duration. This sleep is a deeper sleep than REM and much less is known of it.
There are those who believe that it is during this phase that we astral travel.
Astral travel is said to occur for all of us during our sleeping periods. This is
hard to prove scientifically, as astral travel may seem like a dream. The astral
realm is much the same as the physical plane and so can be hard to identify,
especially if we do not understand what is happening. Again, there are books
on the subject, including those that claim to give a practical way to identify
astral travel and to have astral projections that we remember and can control.

What is certain and scientifically proven is that we need both types of sleep:
REM and deep sleep. We crave sleep still, even if we have had some sleep,
but only of one type. We need to dream and we need to astral travel, or deep
sleep, whichever it is that occurs. We can only do both if we have adequate
sleep. Therefore I say we should make sure we get at least 7 hours of sleep
every night for proper functioning of the body and mind. If we have trouble
sleeping, it is often because our mind is full of the stuff that happened

throughout the day. This is where the benefits of meditation come in, an hour of meditation before we go to bed, allows our mind to unwind from the day and let us sleep by the time we get to bed. Watching TV late into the night does not make for good sleep. Our dreams are more likely to be troubled by the programme we were watching. Dreams are often valid expressions of the mind's problem-solving techniques, it is often said if we have a problem to "sleep on it". Many inventors and scientists solved their problems through dreams, and it is so for us "ordinary" folk too.

So, make sure you get some good sleep tonight!

Action Points

- Start exercising physically, anything, just do it!
- Decide to do some mental exercise also
- Try to have good and/or enjoyable sex at least 3 times a week
- Start meditation
- Get a good 7 hours of sleep every night

<u>Diet and Nutrition</u>

The solar plexus chakra is yellow and relates to the "gut instincts". It is about personal power, self-esteem and creating boundaries. It allows the transmutation of emotions, eg from anger into action. It represents personality and building and releasing energy. It also represents the digestive system. The Warrior of the Rainbow must work to keep themselves healthy and having a good diet is the best way forward. Having a healing diet is the best thing you can do for your body and your planet. We all need to eat.

You Are What You Eat

This has always been true, but never has it been more of an issue than the last 5 – 10 years or so. With the advent of "food crises" such as GM foods and pandemics caused by eating animals; what we eat has never been so dangerous. The government is becoming more and more concerned with the nation's health and it seems that no one knows how to eat right anymore. With an aging population in the West, never have we been in the situation where there are more people over 50 years old than under 50 years old. Therefore what we eat becomes increasingly important, if we are to live healthily into old age, rather than becoming a burden on the health system.

It is said that cows eating prions from diseased sheep's brains cause BSE. It is rarely questioned whether the practice of feeding a vegetarian animal flesh which it does not have the intestinal capacity to deal with, was ever really a smart idea. There are also many who believe that BSE is in fact caused by organo-phosphate poisonings – spraying our food with agrichemicals (Or rather agrochemicals, as I like to call them!). It may well be that Parkinson's and Alzheimer's are the human equivalent and that years of eating pesticide, herbicide and fungicide will take its toll on the body and produce bizarre health conditions, not previously known on this planet.

It should be remembered that these agrochemicals were originally designed as chemical weapons for World War II. I have to say that I do not find the idea that weapons of mass destruction should be sprayed over the food I eat either sensible, scientific or tolerable. As the various insects and weeds adapt over generations to tolerate these deadly chemicals, companies such as Aventis, Du Pont, and Monsanto (now bought out by Bayer) try to come up with ever more destructive and deadly chemicals to combat the "farmer's enemy". We are told again and again that the farmer must use this assortment of assaults on nature, because the population is increasing so much and food production is hard pushed to keep up with it.

However, the truth is that never in the Planet's history has so much food been produced - plenty enough to feed the world – yet every **day** 10,000 children die of starvation and related causes. 854 million people are undernourished and a further 100 million are living below the poverty line and have neither the land to grow food or the money to buy it. Yet also, in Western civilisation, our landfill sites are crammed with uneaten food. Whether it is because the food was bought and never cooked, or because the restaurants over-filled the plates so you could feel you were getting "value for money" or the supermarket did not sell it before the "best before" date. Yet this very same food is often covered with poison for our body's natural systems.

Our bodies evolved to eat starchy grains, root vegetables, a very small amount of stringy meat with a proportionate amount of fat, fresh fruits, berries and green leafy veggies. Few people in the Western world follow this diet today (yes, even the paleo people have it in the wrong proportions) and so we have an incredible array of cancers, gout, nervous diseases and heart conditions which are killing us at younger and younger ages. Meanwhile, the same companies that sought to continue their profits on chemical weapons are running out of ideas and patents on those chemicals. Now the "best way" to combat weeds, insects and food shortages is with GM foods.

A Genetically Modified food is one where an ingredient of that food has had an implantation of alien DNA spliced into its cells. The purpose for which is to make the plant growing immune to herbicide, or pesticide. Therefore, the plant can now be sprayed with said herbicide or pesticide; so more chemicals are used, not less! Also, just for good measure, all these plants have a gene for tolerance to antibiotics. It is used as a marker gene, so that scientists can tell that the gene splicing worked. As doctors are fast running out of useful antibiotics and there is an upsurge in their usage, this seems very strange to play about with the possibility that such a gene may be passed on in the gut, thus rendering our own immune systems open to viral invasion. There seems to be only profit motivating the development of these plants and you must realise that whoever controls the world's food supplies, controls the world.

We can't eat oil or gold!

Again we are lied to about the safety and efficacy of these novel food plants. There is no harm in eating DNA, we are told; we do it all the time. Yes, but not usually the gene from a petunia! These foods are "substantially equivalent" to the original plants, we are told. Yet studies of German honeybees have shown that the plant's GM DNA is taken up in the bee's guts. The bees become sick and die. Is it necessary to take the risk that the same will not happen to humans? This is the question not being asked, whilst Aventis, Du Pont and Bayer again push their unwanted poisons onto an unsuspecting public. Just so that their shareholders can continue to make huge profits. This is what counts for these companies. They are not interested in feeding the world. If they were, they would divert some of their billions to ensure that a healthy food supply was available for those starving millions in the Developing World.

And it is not just GM foods that we need to worry about. The fact is that without two vital things, there will be no food for any of us. Without pollinating insects or soil bacteria nothing can grow. It is true that some plants such as wheat use the wind for pollination, but even wheat needs the soil bacteria. As a child I remember driving to Brighton from Wokingham and the car windscreen would be covered with splatted flying insects. Now, anywhere we drive it is only rarely that the windscreen is insect splatted. It wasn't pleasant, these insects splatting on the windscreen, I would hate it each time it happened. It seems to me indicative though, of how the pesticides have finally done their damage. Killed off so many insects, good and bad indiscriminately, I wonder how many years we have left before there are too few. Herbicides are responsible for the demise of the soil bacteria, in particular glyphosate is the main culprit. Made by our old friends Monsanto, readily available to the consumer as well as the farmer. I am not a soil scientist, I have no idea how the numbers of soil bacteria have changed over time, I have no idea how long we have left before there are too few. I doubt we even know how few is too few.

It has been calculated that it would cost somewhere between US$7 and $265 billion to end world hunger, yet the US military budget is over $600 billion a year. A military that is already far bigger than all the rest of the world's force put together.

We can see that it is not largely lack of food that kills the starving populations of this world – it is more to do with a lack of money, lack of profit to anyone and lack of political will. Anyone who denies this or tries to say otherwise is not looking at the evidence. In the West we throw away tons of food each year, we even buy food from countries where people are starving. Work that one out!

We are one planet, we are one people.

We are all just ever-changing patterns of energy. To hurt another is to hurt ourself. One day soon, we are going to come to this realisation. If we do not, we are going to destroy this planet, our home and all who live on her - which obviously includes ourselves. Saving the planet is the most selfish thing anyone could do.

We are what we eat – therefore if you wish to have a healthy body that is capable of carrying your soul for 80 years or more (and the body was designed to last more like 120 years) – you will have to eat healthy food. This may well require some major re-thinking and re-organisation on your part. However, if you are reading this book at all, then you must be interested in keeping your body in a healthful condition for it's long life. What you eat affects your mind and emotions as well as your body. Many people become grouchy if their blood sugar falls too low. This is easily noticed by people and can be easily remedied. There are other more subtle influences that food has on the emotions too. Perhaps many forms of depression and other mental illnesses can be radically improved with a change in diet. Something that not many doctors consider.

What is healthy food? It is food that your body was designed to eat and knows how to digest. It is food that is free from toxins and pollutants. It is 'natural' food.

To eat healthy food: First it must be organic. If you eat foods that are produced by the factory-farm method, you are polluting your own body with toxins that it was never designed to handle and unwittingly contributing towards the pollution of the soil and water; soil erosion, algal blooms, destruction of the rainforests and the extinction of half the species on this planet.

"Hang on, I only wanted a cheap loaf of bread", you say- yet if you look back to pre-WWII and how much people spent on food then; you will see that it is very different to how much we spend now. Pre-WWII, we spent approximately 40% of our income on food, these days it is more like 12%. We need to accept that if we spent more like 25% of our income on food, we would live much healthier lifestyles – both for our planet and ourselves.

Organic food is produced without the use of synthetic pesticides or herbicides that our bodies cannot tolerate. This also means that organically produced animals are not subjected to routine administrations of anti-biotics given to most farm animals due to the over-crowded conditions that they habitually live in.

Biodynamic food is also produced organically and additionally with regard to the health of the soil. Biodynamics is a science of life-forces, a recognition of the basic principles at work in nature, and an approach to agriculture which takes these principles into account to bring about balance and healing. In a very real way, then, Biodynamics is an ongoing path of knowledge rather than an assemblage of methods and techniques. Biodynamics recognizes that soil itself can be alive, and this vitality supports and affects the quality and health of the plants that grow in it. Therefore, one of Biodynamics fundamental efforts is to build up stable humus in our soil through composting.

Truly the Earth sustains us. Without soil bacteria, nothing on this planet would be able to grow – yet agrochemicals and GM foods actually destroy soil bacteria. Please think about that, the next time you spray "Round-up" on your lawn. Chemical agriculture has developed short-cuts to quantity by adding soluble minerals to the soil. The plants take these up via water, thus by-passing their natural ability to seek from the soil what is needed for health, vitality and growth. The result is a deadened soil and artificially stimulated growth. We must ensure we buy certified organic or transitional foods. Transitional foods are those that are grown organically, but cannot yet be called organic as the soil has still been contaminated with agrochemicals. A 3 year transitional period is needed for food to be certified organic. One of the major barriers to more farmers becoming organic is the 3-year transitional period. During this time, they cannot sell their produce as organic and so they lose money during this period. As you can imagine, 3 years is a long time to not make ends meet, hence many farmers simply cannot afford to go down this route. Many also find that initially their yields also decrease. However, once this time is over, using organic techniques, the farmer is soon able to recoup the yields gained previously through agrochemical use.

It would be great if farming subsidies were used to support farmers through transitional years, rather than paying them not to grow particular crops or raise particular animals.

Once we are buying organic food – if possible from a farm shop or farmer's market, which reduces the amount of transportation the produce goes through, think about how else we might reduce our impact on this planet. Any food straight from the ground is preferable to that which has been picked, packed and sent off 100s of miles to a central distribution centre (where it may sit for a few days!) then sent out hundreds of miles to all the shops. A food that has been transported in this way has lost much of its energy and therefore its health-giving properties. In the UK, most of the organic food sold in supermarkets is pre-packed in plastic – it seems a total anathema to me. Plastic is one of the deadliest products used on a regular basis in our current society and here we go wrapping our healthiest food in it! It is quite bizarre and shows that the supermarkets have quite lost the plot and do not have any understanding of the process at all. Best way we can save our planet in the short term is to buy as local as possible. I know we're all into the habit of doing the weekly shop at the supermarket – a one-stop shop and getting everything we need all in one go. Time to take our lives back! Demand more of our own time in them. Buy the kids a bicycle -– get them cycling to their piano lessons! Demand safe cycle routes from our local council so we feel OK with doing this.

Back to buying our organic veggies from the farm-shop, ideally or even growing our own – but more on that later. Choose the freshest-looking veggies and buy what you enjoy eating. You may be surprised how good natural food actually tastes without salt, sauces or other strong flavours added to them. What I am about to recommend is going to seem extreme to most of us, but all I say is try it for a month. Or even 3.

Cut out from your diet all refined white sugars and flours, all alcohol, all dairy products, all refined grains, all wheat products and all caffeine.
Now you probably think you have nothing left to eat!

If this is so, it just goes to show how poor the current diet is. Start reading the labels on packets – better yet – don't buy things that come in packets! Revert to a diet closer to what our ancestors ate. We will notice a difference. At first you may find that you suffer from headaches or pains, or other symptoms of detoxification such as fever, fatigue, skin eruptions, emotional irritability, gas, temporary constipation or diarrhea, temporary stopping of menstruation, yawning or even tight muscles.

Do not worry. It is your body starting to be able to remove all the toxins that it has been accumulating for the last 20, 30, 40 years. I know it will be tempting to give in and have a jam doughnut or whatever… but <u>do</u> try to stay off these foods. It will not be easy - a sign that these foods are almost as addictive as heroin. If you are like me, these foods will have been what you grew up with. We ate them unquestioningly, as our mothers fed us them. Herself, no doubt also brought up to believe it is OK to eat these poisons. However, just because our parents and grandparents ate this way, does not necessarily make it good. What have our elder relatives died of? Cancer? Diabetes? Heart attack? None of these are 'natural' causes at all. They are very much unnatural causes, caused by living on a toxic planet, eating a poor diet that our bodies were never designed to cope with.

When we start this toxic-free diet, we may find our energy levels plummet at first. This again, is a sign of toxic overload. Please do not be fooled into thinking that the remedy is a handful of chocolate. Ride the symptoms out. Try to detox as a family, or with our neighbours or friends; that way we will have support when we need it and want/crave that doughnut or cream cake. And if chocolate is really what you desire, then try cacoa nibs or a dark chocolate (min. 72% cacoa) instead

How to combat our lack of energy: I recommend spirulina. It costs less than 50p per day and if we don't think that we are worth even that little, why bother with any of this? The Amazonian superfood maca is also great to add in smoothies as a powder or take as a supplement in capsules. Tai chi or yoga are good for energy boosts. There are also natural energy-boosting plants such as ginseng and guarana.

Let me tell you the story of how I became raw vegan from being vegetarian for 14 years.

I thought I had a pretty healthy lifestyle, being vegetarian and eating mostly organic. Then, during an operation it was discovered that I had endometriosis. Now this is a disease that is being found more often. As we pollute our world more and more and move further away from natural living, we help it increase. With this problem, the cells inside the uterus decide to grow elsewhere. They cover the ovaries, possibly also the bladder, the bowels, they have been found as far away as the heart and the brain! Pretty serious stuff! I had always had extremely painful periods and now I knew why. I read lots of books about the problem. Most of them gave me no hope. Even with surgery, the cells would replace themselves within 3 – 5 years! As you can imagine, it was not what I wanted to hear. However, many of the books said that many of the symptoms could be relieved with a change of diet. I had been reading about PMS as well and those books also recommended very similar changes of diet. I thought what could I lose other than painful periods every month?

I stopped refined sugars and flours, alcohol, wheat, dairy, refined grains and citrus. (OK, I confess, I couldn't go all the way and give up coffee or chocolate; both organic, the chocolate, vegan and made with raw sugar cane) Nevertheless, I was stunned at the difference! I cut out dairy first, as this was the easiest for me. My next period had halved my intense pain to one day, instead of two! Incredible! Next out were alcohol, sugars and wheat. This brought my PMS to almost zero! Absolutely amazing! Just from changing my diet for a month. If we have eaten something all our life, it is impossible to tell if it is bad for us until we stop eating it for a few weeks. I even found the colour of my menstrual blood changed – from dark, dark red to a bright, oxygenated red. Now, instead of spending my period days curled up in bed, in too much agony to move (with or without the use of painkillers) I can get on with my day. It is almost like any other day, except I feel a bit heavier. I can get some pain, but the use of paracetamol stops it. Previously I had been through stages of trying different non-steroidal anti-inflammatories every month, none of which actually worked ("Can't let you have anything stronger, we don't want you becoming addicted" as the doctors would all tell me). Now I am mostly raw and vegan; my periods are so easy! I am no longer desperate for menopause!

Why raw? After starting such a restrictive diet I found I was basically just eating fruits and vegetables, nuts and seeds. I realised that as my diet was so restrictive, I needed to get the most nutrition out of it as I could. When anything is cooked, it starts to degrade, so basically if you eat it raw – you are going to get the most nutrition out of it as possible. The only exceptions to this are carrots and potatoes – which ideally should be cooked a very little to release their nutrients. I find that carrot juice or grated carrot is good enough. Potatoes are slowing to the detox process anyway, so I don't eat them very often.

The most highly nutritious and healthful foods are sprouts! Yeah! Yuk! I hear you all saying not sprouts. Let me also say that I refer here to fresh sprouted seeds and beans, not brussel sprouts. Boring! Well if that is your opinion; please try to rethink it. Sprouts are tasty, highly nutritious and are the raw enzymes from the plant's DNA. They are absolutely fabulous for us and if you really don't like them, try using delicious dressings! Yes! Coconut milk, avocado and raw tahini with a bit of garlic, ginger, parsley or coriander is so sumptuous you will wonder why you haven't been eating them for years! Sprinkle a few sunflower seeds and cashew nuts over the top – wow! Delicious! And incredibly cheap!

Would I lie to you?

If our energy levels have been low, sprouts are the things to pick us up again and restore our good humour! Yes, it's true. They can even cheer up our soul! As can plums, nature's natural source of serotonin, the "happy" neurotransmitter in the brain.

Plant enzymes are vital to our body's well-being. They can directly replace the amino acids our body uses in its daily processes of keeping our cells alive and functioning.

I am not suggesting that every person on the planet should become raw vegans overnight. That would be unlikely and not in the best interests of most. Start slow. Try to build up the amount of raw food that we eat. It does not have to be salad. Most people's idea of salad is very poor, in any case. Salads are not just tomatoes, iceburg lettuce and cucumbers. Salads do not even have to contain any green leafy veggies. My salads are spinach or kale with grated carrots, sweet potatoes, beetroot or parsnips, sweet corn, radishes, mushrooms, nuts and seeds (especially hemp seeds, which are high in protein and contain gamma linoleic acids) and sprouts, finished with a dressing of avocado, coconut milk and garlic base. Or variations thereof.

Try to increase our intake of raw food to 50% per day. We can still eat the food we like, just bolster it with raw food. (Organic, please) Having carrots? Leave them raw, just grate them on the side. Chopping the food small can often make it more palatable, as does pouring delicious sauces over it. Never use frozen veg for this. Eating unfrozen veggies would put you off raw food for life. Once something is frozen, its structure is changed and it is never the same once thawed.

Almost any vegetable is able to be eaten raw, many peas are also suitable for raw consumption, but beans and grains are not; they must first be sprouted, neither are meat products, with the exception of some fish, as any sushi place will tell you.

Experiment with your food. Allow it to become interesting again. Most of all, have fun!

A word on dairy: don't. *But it's full of calcium, isn't it?* Well yes, it is full of calcium, but not in a form the body can use! To be able to utilise calcium, there must also be vitamin D and magnesium, it must be chelated (ie have other compounds around it) otherwise it will not be absorbed. The calcium in milk is not chelated and milk does not have magnesium in it. The calcium in milk is only 12% absorbed! Choral calcium has the best absorption rates and it goes straight to your bones as the choral is similar to your bone structure. It has even been hypothesized that milk will degrade calcium from your body.

There are many diets hypothesized and many of them work, many of them fail to work. Question is do people really follow them? Diets tend not to work as people get bored of them and go back to their previous eating habits. The only diet that works is to keep to our eating habit. Entrench it in our system. We do not have to be extreme, but there is a difference between eating some chocolate once a month and eating it every day.

Buy a juicer and start experimenting with fruit and vegetable juices. There are many books on the subject now. It's a good way to introduce raw food into your diet.

Humans are naturally happy creatures – watching any 2-year-old should convince you of this. If we are not happy I would attribute much of it to our lifestyle, with a large emphasis on diet. I find that just 2 days of only eating cooked food is enough to get me depressed. My energy levels drop and I start feeling miserable. One bowl of salad later and I am back up! If that doesn't tell us something, I don't know what does!

We would like to utilise organic food but we can't afford it? Then grow our own! Yes, really! Whether we have a garden or not. Many town councils are crying out for people to use their allotments and they can be extremely reasonably priced. "I don't have the time for that!" I hear you cry. Growing plants using the permaculture method is precisely designed so that we don't have to spend much time on our veggie patch.

"What's permaculture?" It's a design system; it can be adapted to anything, not just growing things. The idea is that we integrate our plants and animals so that one system feeds another and the whole thing becomes totally sustainable. If you are fortunate to own your own home and garden, you can take the whole design a step further. I would recommend going into the local library and hunting down Bill Mollison's Introduction to Permaculture book. Much of Mollison's may not be applicable to you, so just read the bits that do apply to you. Even better, many adult education colleges offer permaculture courses these days. Find one in your area and do it.

Basically, we will need to find out what grows well in the soil type we have. Ask other allotmenters. Most root and salad veggies will grow almost anywhere, so we probably will not have too many restrictions. There are also many books in our library about growing our own veggies and some of these may even be regionally specific. Meanwhile, you can start composting. There are many types of composter available these days. I would recommend a worm farm. These incredible creatures will eat any organic matter and turn it into good, nutrient-rich soil – ideal if your current soil type is quite sandy or clay-laden. Thus, you can spend the winter turning your allotment or garden into workable soil. Alternatively collect orange boxes. Fill up the boxes with your organic waste and stack them one on top of the other. By the time you have 5 or so, the bottom one will be good to use.

Start small and easy and work your way up. Anyone can grow carrots, onions, potatoes and courgettes. They grow very easily with virtually no interference. Just plant and watch. Start with herbs on your window-sill.

To avoid pests – grow your veggies interspersed with each other. Mix your carrots, onions and potatoes all in one patch. Scatter your lettuces, kales and courgettes throughout. The cabbage moth recognises its food from the long straight rows that they are planted in. Therefore plant them in random patterns and you eliminate this pest. Same idea with the carrot fly, which sniffs out its prey at a remarkable distance. Hide your carrots amongst strong smelling veggies such as onions and garlics. Force the carrot fly to eat your fellow allotmenters' veggies instead.

Allotments are great places to hide from the family, or even better, spend time with the family! Get your children interested in the miracle of growing their own organic food! You will be surprised how much can be grown and will be joyfully sharing your produce with your neighbours and work colleagues. You never know, you might even get a second income from it eventually?

If you feel particularly adventurous and you enjoy meditating (or do after reading more of this book!) – you might want to try combining the two. Meditate in your veggie patch. Sit close to your veggies and imagine sending them energy. It doesn't matter whether you believe in what you're doing or not, but you may be surprised to find your veggies growing larger and tastier than your neighbour's. Give it a go.. what have you got to lose?

Only poor health.

All I am saying is we should not allow ourselves to be completely dependent on the supermarkets for our food. We need to start growing our own, even if it's just a few herbs on the windowsill.

Eat our way to health. Drink and smoke less, exercise more.

Just do it.

<u>Action Points</u>

- Eat Organic
- Introduce raw food into our diet
- Avoid refined white flours, sugars and grains
- Avoid alcohol and caffeine
- Drink fresh, squeezed juices instead
- Start growing our own food
- Buy local produce from a farmer's market or farm shop
- Decrease our reliance on dairy products

Love

The heart chakra is green and is unconditional love. It is about opening up to the Universal Love, it is the gateway to the Spiritual Self. Its element is air and it takes the impact of the emotions. It represents the thymus, heart, lungs and arms. The Warrior must open their heart and let the Universal Love in as well as give out love to others too. The Warriors of the Rainbow aspire to love everyone unconditionally. It is important to give love and to receive love from other beings. These beings may be animal, human or spiritual. Every person on the planet has access to spiritual love whenever they need it.

Love is a four-letter word!

It is one of the most underused words in the English language. It is one of our deepest emotions, yet also one of the most mysterious. What causes us to "fall in love"? There are many theories about this. All I can say is that the more you love, the more you love! As the song says:

"Love is something if you give it away, give it away, give it away;

Love is something if you give it away, you end up having more"

We all need love. It is one of the most binding things about humans. It is not difficult to see the disastrous results that occur when we are not loved. And it is not just humans that need love.. it extends to all life. Yes, even the goldfish with its famed 6-second memory needs love. There are many anecdotes of fish that have died very quickly after their tank-mate died.

Dogs pine for their owners – if the owner dies first.

How many times do you hear that a person "died of a broken heart"? Quite often.

Love is a very special emotion. Its opposite hate, does not have the same effect. No one died of hatred. Hatred is negative love – you hate because you love. It is the same emotion expressed in a negative way. How often do you hear that "love turned to hate". How many couples do you know of who were "so in love" but after splitting up, "hate each other". They do not really hate – they still love each other, but can no longer express that love in a positive way.

There are many beliefs about love – the love you feel for your parents is different from the love you feel for your partner. The love you have for a cat or dog is different from the love you have for your child. When you first "fall in love", it is different from the long-term love that then develops afterwards. Love is also an action, not just an emotion. It can be passive, it can also be forceful, it can change your life. When you finally meet your soulmate, the emotions and feelings unleashed are incredible. Very strong, very powerful. Love can change the world too.

Love is also an ever-changing pattern of energy. We have little idea of what causes it. There is much talk of pheromones – the hormones that attract us to each other. Yet no understanding of why one person's pheromones attract you but another person's doesn't. Is it all just physical? Perhaps there are spiritual elements also? Maybe the person you love in this life is the same entity as someone you loved in a previous life?

Love and sex are connected, yet also entirely different. You can love a person without having sex with them and have sex with a person you don't love. But when sex and love do meet, it is fantastic! The heights of pleasure that can be reached are amazing.

Make love, not war

This was the old 1960's saying and I still believe the world would be a happier place if all our political leaders had a truly loving relationship with their partners. Unfortunately ambition and greed get in the way and our leaders do not understand the true concept of power. They believe it to be a force originating from outside themselves and feel they must take it from others, rather than feeling it within their own beings.

Look at Tibet. Tibetans, like the Native American Indians, had tales and prophecies of the time when they would be invaded. For them also, it is a test. Each individual living during the take-over there had chosen to be there at that time. To test themselves, perhaps? To take the opportunity to really see if they could stand up for what they believed in, even under the greatest adversity, without resort to violence. And so it still is.

You can begin to see that love and power are also linked. "The power of love" is often talked about. Love does have the power to conquer all, which is why I include a chapter about it in this book. We all need and crave love, some perhaps more than others. Love is never-ending, it is all encompassing, it can override all other emotions … there are so many tales of the power of love.

"All you need is Love", sang The Beatles and it is true.

Psychologists have conducted experiments on monkeys that seem to indicate that they prefer love to food: baby monkeys are separated from their mothers and placed in small rooms with wire-cage monkey dummies. One is bare wires and milk, the other is covered with terry cloth. The baby monkeys spend more of their time with the terry-cloth dummy, going to the milk-laden one only for feeding. This seems to indicate that the monkeys would rather be loved and nurtured than fed. We can extrapolate this behaviour to humans also.

Thus if you cannot love your enemy; you should at least feed them. Hate is a different aspect of love. You cannot hate someone or something that you do not care about. The person will have no effect on you if you do not love them or expect love from them. If you hate a parent, partner or indeed, humanity; it is because you love that parent, partner or humanity.

We tend to idealise our loved ones, so when they fall short of our ideal it is easy for us to let our emotions turn to hate or anger.

Love is the strongest emotion and like everything else in our Universe; it is not static. It is dynamic; it is also ever changing energy and so the nature of our love for a person or our planet changes. Over time, love becomes deeper and stronger. We love our partners and friends because they represent some ideal way of being that we ourselves aspire to.

Love. We all need it, we all crave it and if we do not get it, we become frustrated. This frustration manifests in a variety of ways. When a whole nation lacks love, then it creates war. Currently the nation that is most lacking in love, is the one with the most capitalist or materialist outlook: The US. War on drugs, war on terrorism, war on any system that is not capitalist, war on prisoners ... The result is that the US has some of the worst violent crime rates per capita in the world.

"Anybody can be a millionaire,

So everybody has to try,

In the heart of this human jungle,

Only the heartless will survive"

as Matt Johnston put it.

It does not have to be this way. If we can all learn to love <u>ourselves</u>, to value ourselves for the important and loving beings that we are; then we can truly love our friends, partners, parents, children, neighbours and enemies.

In the film "The Fifth Element", an alien being is transported to Earth to become part of an experiment to transform us all. This Fifth Element is love. We are all the Fifth Element; if only we would realise it.

I believe that I am on this planet to learn how to love others. I am here to learn to love all beings. It is not easy. There are many people who do not allow their emotions free reign, who are scared to love and be loved. They have loved and been hurt in the past. It takes too long to recover. Best not to get involved in the first place.

So many people in so much pain … I want to hug and hold them all. I want to love them all better. I want to show what is possible.

What can I do? What can any of us do?

Just keep on loving, no matter what. If you are rejected, keep loving. If you are hurt, keep loving. I love deeply and am hurt easily – aren't we all? I would rather love and be loved and be so happy with the highs than never love and keep myself isolated and "safe" from hurt, safe from love too. Experience the joys of loving and being loved. We are here on this planet to love and bring joy to others. It is possible to put aside the hurt, to open our heart, to allow love to enter.

Yes, we will get hurt but the pain goes away everything is all just ever-changing patterns of energy if we do not dwell and brood, we will recover and be happy again.

No one is always 100% happy, conversely, no one is 100% miserable. We swing from one to the other as our moods and emotions take us and it is ok.

This is life.

This is what it is all about!

Love yourself. This is the first lesson, if we do not love ourselves unconditionally, forgive ourselves our wrongs, we cannot love another. This is the problem with the world. We are looking to someone else to forgive us, but only we can do it. Not one of our priests can do it, only us. We have to make our peace with ourselves, before we can make peace with our Maker. The first part of love is acceptance. Once we can accept the humanness of ourselves or another maybe we can forgive our or their behaviour. This can be the first step to loving.

We are travellers on a cosmic journey -

stardust swirling and dancing in the eddies and whirlpools of infinity

Life is Eternal

But the expressions of Life are ephemeral, momentary, transitory.

We have stopped for a moment to encounter each other;

to meet, to Love, to share.

This is a precious moment - a parenthesis in Eternity -

but it is transient.

If we share with lightheartedness, caring and Love,

we will create abundance and joy for each other.

And then this moment will have been worthwhile

- Accept ourselves for who we are
- Love ourselves as we would another
- Love all those in our life, whether we "get on" with them, or not
- Start with acceptance

Self- Awareness

The throat chakra is blue and is the expression of the Self. It is about creativity, manifesting your goals in the physical world. Live an ideal Life, be surrounded by beauty, have control over your own mental abilities. Its watchword is "My deepest Truth". The Rainbow Warrior needs to speak their own Truth. To find out what is your own truth, one needs to investigate the self. Who am I? What is my purpose? Why am I here?

It is said that humans are the only species on the planet capable of self-awareness. Supposedly the only creatures who are aware of their own mortalities are ourselves. Personally, I am not convinced.

How do scientists know this? They don't! After all, if you came across a people whose language you did not understand, but merely observed them … how, exactly would they differ in their behaviour from primates, dolphins, whales etc?

I believe it is our inability to fully understand the world we live in and the animal species that we share it with, which leads certain scientists to come to such arrogant conclusions.

Many of us have pets and can attest to very different personalities within dogs, cats, horses etc. What is personality if it isn't a measure of self-awareness? (Amongst other things) Therefore, I believe many creatures on this Planet are self-aware and many of them could teach us a thing or two. If only we would listen! Another question I always ask myself is: if humans are supposed to be the clever species, why do we insist on teaching animals how to talk like us, instead of learning the language of the animals?

What is self-awareness and how do we become more self-aware? To become more self-aware; we need to examine our nature and our beliefs. Why do we do the things we do? Why do we feel certain emotions at certain times? Do you enjoy all aspects of your behaviour? Does everyone else?

Answering these questions will lead you into greater self-awareness. Do not think that having answered them we can sit back and relax, having perfectly understood ourselves. We will find that our answers change over time and change with new experiences. We are all ever-evolving beings in the process of becoming.

What does that mean? It means we are in this three dimensional physical experience to learn and understand that our energy, as it is translated into feelings, thoughts and emotions causes all our experience. **There are no exceptions**. Things do not "just happen" to us. We create our own experience. Our emotions follow our beliefs – it is not the other way around. If you do not believe this – examine some positive beliefs you have that you are happy with. Trace how your emotions follow these beliefs. For example: I have the belief that I do not want a boring Life. I believe that I am positive-thinking. As a result, I am usually a happy person. Mostly my feelings are positive. There are times when I am not happy, but I know that this feeling will change. I know I should eat a good raw salad or have some figs or dates. My emotions do not stay depressed for long. My life is very interesting and I do not know what I am doing from one month to the next. It is not the sort of life most people would want, but it is how I want to live. And it works for me. Understand that we can all do the same with new beliefs we wish to bring into our life.

If you wish to learn more about yourself in a more structured way enrol yourself in a Counselling Skills course. Even if you do not "need" these skills in your professional life, what is taught during such a course is usually invaluable for learning about yourself.

I believe we are on this planet to evolve spiritually until we learn to understand ourselves fully and accept that it is all just ever-changing patterns of energy. Once we can reach this stage, we will be ready to live in peace and harmony with our fellow beings.

However, before we get there, we need to take personal responsibility for ourselves.

What does that mean? It means that you accept that you are responsible for your life. You and nobody else. Most of us are happy to accept personal responsibility for the positive things that happen to us. e.g. getting a promotion is the result of our dedication and hard work to the job.

Much fewer of us are willing to accept personal responsibility for the bad things that happen to us. Please note at this point that there is a major difference between taking personal responsibility and blaming yourself. If you blame yourself, then you make yourself a victim – if you take personal responsibility, you understand why this bad thing happened to you and you don't make yourself a victim. There is always a lesson to be learned from the "negative" events in our lives. e.g. Getting your home burgled may be the result of not paying attention to security. No point in blaming yourself here, it won't bring your possessions back. Perhaps it is a lesson to help you understand that your possessions are just things. How often do you hear of a burglary and the person cries out, not over the stolen stereo, but the trinket that belonged to their grandmother. Such happenings occur for a reason. Not to take things for granted, perhaps? Many different reasons. This is what we need to determine when we experience a "negative" event. What lesson are we learning from it? Sometimes it can be hard to determine and often there is likely to be more than one.

Personal responsibility is a lifestyle choice. It enables us to take control of our life. We have no need to feel like a victim, or that our parents, teachers, partner or boss runs our life, or that they are to blame for it. You are in control and always will be. We need to remember that no matter what other people will tell you – it is your life, no one else can live it for you and no one else can – or indeed will - take responsibility for it. If more people took personal responsibility for their lives and the effects of their lives and chose to do what they wanted with their lives instead of what they felt they should – then this world would be a much happier place.

Whilst we are on the subject of personal responsibility, you might be relieved to know that everyone of us is responsible for our own deaths. It stands to reason that we must all die, we cannot live forever in the same physical body and nor would we want to! We might be scared of our own death... but that is not the same as wanting to live forever. Many people hold the belief that to be old is to be decrepit, useless and of no value. Such people may then die whilst they are still young. They may not choose the exact date and time of death in this plane of existence, but they do choose to "go out with a bang". Perhaps they are caught in a natural or man-made disaster.

No one dies who does not choose to do so

How many of us do a job we do not like because we feel we have to in order to pay off the mortgage? Most people in Western society. This is not living! Where is our creative energy being expressed? If you can answer that question – that's excellent. Many people cannot. Many people believe they do not have any creative energy. This is simply not true. We all have it – how it is or can be expressed is entirely up to each of us. Being creative does not mean we have to excel in it. We can simply paint for the pleasure it gives us, we do not need to paint a masterpiece.

What moves us? Find the answer to that and we have some idea of where our creative energy lies.

How to express it? Just do it! Paint, draw, write, dance, sing, play an instrument, laugh, anything.

Who are you? Ask yourself this question every 6 months or so. Write down the answers and watch how they change. If they do not; what are you doing with your life? Are you happy with that?

Increase your conscious awareness of yourself. Take up a Counselling Skills course or read Carl Rogers or Jane Roberts. These authors open our eyes, heart and mind to the beings that we are.

I believe we are all beings of light, focussed in this three dimensional physical plane to learn certain lessons before moving on to the next stage of consciousness. There is no limit to the number of physical lifetimes a being can enjoy. Just because this part of you is experiencing a physical life on Planet Earth, does not mean that there are not other parts of your being currently experiencing other forms of reality.

Another way to increase our conscious awareness of our being is through meditation. Meditation is a small word which covers a multitude of exercises. There are many ways to meditate and some of these are explained in more detail in the chapter on Daily Exercise.

If we accept that we are ever-changing patterns of energy (like everything else in this universe) at the very core of our being, then perhaps we can accept that, as such, we can influence all energy in the universe. Think about the way you influence other people e.g. do you offer a positive aspect to their lives? Do you inspire them to be more creative or enjoy themselves more? Or do you make those around you become sober and sullen? Do people start cowering in your presence? Such behaviour on their part is not a show of power in yourself. It is in fact a show of weakness. Encourage others to become the best that they can be, don't frustrate and limit them to negative behaviour patterns. Given ideal conditions, everyone will improve and shine in the glory of their own being – at which point, we are making the most of other people; instead of the least.

If you are a person cowering from your boss, it's time to stop being a victim and become responsible for yourself. Even if this eventually means that you leave your job or are sacked. It can only lead on to bigger and better ways of being.

"Do what makes you happy and the rest will follow" someone once told me and it is true.

We all create our own reality. There are certain "rules" we agree to live by on this planet, such as we agree that although everything is all just ever-changing patterns of energy (ask a quantum physicist if you don't believe me) we cannot pass our arms through the apparently solid table. We also agree to experience time as a series of related events that follow each other – whereas certain physicists will tell you that all time is happening now.

What this means is that if there is a part of our life that we are not happy with – we can change it. We are not powerless – though there are those who would have us believe otherwise. The point of power is in the present – when our non-physical self merges with corporal reality. The recognition of that fact alone can revitalise our life. If we accept this to be true … there is nothing we cannot create for ourselves. The future starts now.

If we are sick – we can make ourselves well and do not listen to those who tell you otherwise. If we feel that we should not die now – we can ensure that we do not. Concentrate on being well. Send yourself the power of your positive beliefs. Tell yourself you are healthy and well every day. Do not dwell on your ill-health and do one small thing that tells you that you are in good health.

If we are poverty-stricken – we can make ourselves have an acceptable standard of living: again do not listen to those who tell you that you deserve your poverty. Do you think you deserve your poverty? At some level you must think this is so if you are experiencing poverty. Listen carefully to your beliefs and they will show you why you are in the position that you are. You can change this simply by telling yourself that you deserve to be wealthy. Have a target of how much you would like in your bank account. Again make some small gesture that you are wealthy, buy a more expensive brand of baked beans, or whatever.

If we are unhappy with our personal relationships – be it with lovers, parents or children – we do have the power to change the nature of these relationships. We can simply start by giving loving energy to those with whom we have the problems. They do not have to know you are doing it. Just send them a loving, green light and watch their behaviour change.

Whatever we are unhappy with in our life we do have the power to change it and we can start right now.

For a period of 5-10 mins a day, concentrate on an aspect of your life you want to change. Word your thoughts so that they are positive. e.g. do not just say "I don't want to be miserable anymore". Such thinking will then concentrate your mind on your belief that you are miserable. Instead say something like: for example, "I deserve to be happy and wealthy. When I live in the country I will be happy, when I work as an IT consultant I will be wealthy". Couch your words so that your mind understands what will make you happy. If you are really not sure, you can simply say "I deserve to be happy and wealthy". Concentrate on the positive. Do this every day for at least a month and you will start to notice differences in your life. Depending on how removed from the present reality your ideal is, will determine how long it takes to create it.

You can also make up a collage of pictures which describe what you want in your life. This is fun and creative as well as being very effective. If you like, you can concentrate on these images as you do the previous exercise.

It took me nearly three years to work out exactly what I would enjoy doing, where I would enjoy doing it and how I should go about making enough money to do it. (Actually it has taken rather longer than that, if you consider that I have spent my entire life working out what I should do with my life!) I'm still not there yet, but it is coming together slowly. All I can really say is "Have faith". Each year new things happen that take me further along the path to my goal. I feel that I can now say that I am doing all the things I want with my life. I seem to have a 10 year gap between wanting and getting, which seems like a long time. Maybe you can be faster!

Believe strongly – at least for those 5–10 mins and then forget about it. Do not question the efficacy of the self-hypnosis. It will work.

Some things it will not work for: if you are asking for the return of a lost limb or removed organ you will not get this. However you can manifest a lost loved one. They will not be in the form that you previously recognised them in, but if your love is still strong they will be returned to you. Again as this is quite a tall order, you may have to wait until your next lifetime but you will be reunited.

If you love your life, then you are already doing an excellent job of reality creation. If you do not love your life, now is the time to start to change it so that you do.

One part of my life that used to cause me big problems was my monthly period. I would have 2 days of pain and be almost bed-bound. I discovered I had endometriosis – a disease that occurs and is present at birth. Incurable, or so I read time and again in books about the subject. I practised the 5–10 mins of self-hypnosis every day – whilst waiting for the train from Utrecht to Amsterdam. I told myself that the cells in and around my womb and ovaries were healthy and always had been. After a month of this, I eagerly awaited my next period, which was due a week later. I could not believe the difference! Almost no pain! Pain that was completely controlled by paracetamol! For the first time in my life of over 20 years of heavy, debilitating periods … I could go to work my first day on! It was unreal! It has revolutionised my life! I have a life again every day of the month! My pre-menstrual symptoms have also close to disappeared! I would say the change was miraculous – except that I know it occurred at least in part due to my self-hypnosis for a month! I also believe that my change in diet helped this hugely and has ensured that the condition does not return.

After this success – back in June 2002 – I have been working on telling myself that I deserve to be happy and wealthy. I have always been happy so the first is not so hard … but I have always lived close to the edge of poverty in some respects (in a Western world view) I cannot just buy anything I want. I have always had food and shelter though and I am happy with this and consider myself lucky – compared to how many people in the world do not have this. I set myself a "target" of having at least £500 in my bank account. Now I believe that I have met a man who truly makes me very happy and my account does not stray below £500 for very long. I am seriously thinking that I should up my target to £5000 and see what happens!

Which leads us to the question: *Do the starving millions create their own reality then?* To which the answer is yes and no. In reality creation, we must also understand that there are nearly 8 billion other people also creating their realities. On one level of consciousness, those of us who choose to be born in countries of known hardship are aware of the difficulties we will face here. This is not meant to imply that we deserve our fate or should not be helped with foreign aid, but we have chosen this life for some reason. Perhaps we recognise that we still need to learn how the physical body works. There is also the probability that the being is also part of a physical life that does have enough food to eat and clean water to drink.

Reality is our ability to collapse Heisenburg's Uncertainty Principle in a particular way. Heisenburg's Uncertainty Principle states that it is not possible to know both the position and momentum of an electron around its atomic nucleus. There is a 90% probability that the electron is close to the nucleus. However there is a 10% probability that the electron is elsewhere. This 10% includes the possibility that a particular electron is in fact on the other side of the universe. This possibility is very improbable - nevertheless it exists, it is not impossible. It has a value. It is possible that the waveform of Heisenburg's Uncertainty Principle can collapse to the value that means the electron is on the other side of the universe. Therefore quantum mechanics is prepared to say that anything is possible. Eastern philosophy also says that anything is possible. The waveform can be collapsed to any value, but some values are more likely than others. Thus if the reality we are trying to create is wildly at odds with some 8 billion other people's realities, we are much more unlikely to be successful. If it is in tune with the reality of those around us, we are far more likely to succeed.

It is also possible to create the more unlikely values through the projection of our mind during an altered state of consciousness. If we have some "help" to create an unusual value, it becomes easier to obtain. Our "reality creation" is stronger than other people's at that time.

Thus if we are to create peace and harmony with all peoples on this planet, most of us have to consciously want this to happen. Currently too many people do not want it, or think that it is not possible. Both are barriers to the reality occurring.

The only person you can change is yourself. We cannot make others hold different beliefs, but we can show them that there are other possibilities and that these possibilities are equally valid.

Many religions seem to cause disharmony by stating that the unbelievers are to be persecuted, or are unworthy. Some religions say that they must be converted, for their own good; very few say that they are to be tolerated or even celebrated for their differences. If there was more tolerance in our views, if dissent was not seen as disempowering, if all people realised their true potential, we would have our peace and harmony on Earth. When we learn to respect ourselves, we will respect others, then we will respect another person's right to be different.

Our beliefs create our realities. If we believe that people are not to be trusted, are wicked and will rip us off; then we are likely to meet people who are not to be trusted, are wicked and will rip us off. If we believe that people are kind, helpful and understanding then we will meet people who are kind, helpful and understanding. Our beliefs create our reality and our reality will then reinforce our beliefs.

Try a different belief for a month. See what happens. What changes occur to your life?

Have you ever wondered why you had a sudden change in plan, which ensured you were out of town when the floods hit? I know I had intended to visit my friend Rick in Prague, but as I was unable to get a train back, I didn't go and missed being involved in the worst floods for 125 years! The Universe, God, Yahweh, Allah, your Guardian Angel, whoever, whatever you call it; there is some outside (or is it an inner?) power or force that looks after each one of us.

It is true that we do not consciously know the time and date of our deaths but death is programmed into our DNA, no doubt. None can escape the death of this physical body that we currently inhabit, so why not believe that we will die as we previously agreed before our birth? Why not believe that everyone who comes into being in this world, has a purpose and does not leave until that purpose has been fulfilled. Try it for a while, you can always change your belief back if you do not like it. We have to at least accept death as being an inevitable part of life. Sooner or later we all come across death. A well-loved family pet, our grandparents, our parents, a best friend, some other relative. All of these deaths can affect us in very different ways. A person who died after a long and happy life died at what most people would consider is the "right time". How we feel about this death is different from how we feel when a person dies suddenly and unexpectedly, dies young.
Even children who die young have much to teach the families that love them.

We often hear stories of how brave a child is whilst undergoing difficult and painful medical therapy: that child is teaching us all the meaning of courage. The family needs to learn such a lesson. No one is born without purpose. We often have trouble deciding what our purpose is. Part of our life's work is to divine our purpose. Or not. It is also possible to live our life and fulfil our life's work and purpose without ever being sure of what it is or was.

If we need to know; we will seek until we find. If we don't need to know, we will just live, enjoy and fulfil our life's destiny.

We are all here to learn particular lessons – that is the purpose of life. I have given this question much thought over my life. It is the belief that pleases me most. It holds the most positive thoughts for me. Otherwise why would the Universe bother to exist? Science is all very well for answering how, but it has never offered much in the way of why. Why does the Universe exist? No answers from science, but the philosophers can have much fun with this.

Everything is all just ever-changing patterns of energy and our purpose is to evolve spiritually until we realise this on an experiential level, only then will we be able to live in peace and harmony with other beings.

Remember:

Your life is yours and you form it.

You are given the gift of the gods

You create your reality according to your beliefs,

Yours is the creative energy that makes your world;

There are no limitations to the self –

Except those you believe in.

You create your Life through the inner power of your being,

Whose source is within you and yet beyond the selves that you know

Use those creative abilities with understanding abandon.

Honour yourself and move through the godliness of your being.

<u>Action Points</u>

- Question ourselves
- Keep questioning ourselves
- Change our negative beliefs for positive ones
- Read about other ways of thinking, of being
- Try some other ways of being
- Enrol in a counselling skills course

JOBS

The brow or third eye chakra is indigo and is about the art of detachment. It is represented by the pituitary, eyes and brain. It is the religious centre of Being. It enables us to feel at One with the Universe. It is about focus of the mind and Truth. It is vital for Warriors to have right living, to have control over the third eye chakra, to be congruent with all we do.

I have made a few references to jobs over the course of this book. It is something that most of us spend most of our lives doing. Many of us are unhappy in them for one reason or another.

There are 24 hours in a day on this planet (well actually only 23 hours, 57 minutes). An "average" person (whatever that is! There being 3 types of average mathematically speaking, mean, medium and the mode) spends 8 hours asleep. That leaves us with 16 to play with. This average person spends an hour commuting to work; door to door; that leaves us with 14; 1 ½ to 2 hours eating, 12. 2 or 3 hours watching TV. 9 or 10 hours. Then there is perhaps just an hour communication with the family – spouse included; which leaves us with 8 or 9 hours, which are usually spent at work. Worryingly we also spend more time watching TV than communicating with our nearest and dearest!

Therefore most people spend more of their time at work, rather than anything else. Work is usually our major contribution to the world, so we should ensure that it is health creating and positive, rather than negative, destructive and creating illness for yourself or others.

Personally I cannot imagine spending my precious lifetime in this manner. I do not believe it is what we are here for. Our lives are precious – even if we have many of them – they are too precious to waste doing something unworthy or with which we are unhappy with. Our unhappiness will eventually leave us in ill-health.

I have spent some of my time doing the whole job thing and it's not something that sits easily with me. In fact, if you were to look at my CV you'd be hard-pressed to find any evidence of a full-time job.

The closest I have come to such a thing was working as the Radio Operator on a Greenpeace ship! Pretty unconventional, I have to admit. Other "jobs" I have done for any persistent length of time (i.e. more than 2 months) include modelling at Art Colleges and in private, teaching tai chi in various Adult

Education Centres; these worked for me because I was mostly my own boss. I have also done my fair share of factory and office work on a very short-term basis. It kills me! I cannot do it. The last factory job I had was at factory that my mother worked at – making ratchet straps. I lasted 3 weeks and knew that I could not continue to do it – not even for 2 months! It was soul-destroying and not worth the money. I'm sorry, but my time on this planet is precious and I value it too highly to waste it doing some dead-end job that I do not value. I finally had to settle somewhere and have a proper job, I spent two years working in an independent health food store, which was good for my values, but very bad for my time. I felt so tied to the shop, couldn't do anything when I wanted, had to book time off in advance etc. I understand that this is true for most people but I am sure it doesn't have to be.

If we have a job that we love, that we feel valued doing, that we believe is worthwhile, that does not contribute to this planet's destruction – then we are fortunate indeed. Count our blessings and thank us for not caving in to other people's ideas of who we should be and what we should do. We are in a minority though. If we are not in such a job – then change it somehow.

What is more important to us? Our physical, emotional and mental health and our personal fulfillment or paying off the mortgage? If we choose our health and personal fulfillment; we are wise indeed and we need to ensure our job is something we enjoy or something we feel valued doing. Alternatively we can work on turning our current job into something that we enjoy or where we feel valued. Perhaps we love our job – but our boss makes us feel belittled, or otherwise undervalued. Do not put up with it. Get together with our fellow workers and do something about it. Often, when we DO stand up for our rights, we can be surprised to find that our boss did not realise s/he treated us in that manner. S/he may even apologise for it. I do understand it is not easy, however. We never got around to confronting the poor communicators on the Greenpeace ships - it was always easier to just bear it, knowing that either you or they were due off soon. Of course as I was doing something that I totally believed in, that in itself helped me to deal with poor behaviour from certain individuals.

If we believe that our job is <u>not</u> worthwhile, or it contributes to the destruction of our planet please stop doing it now.

Yes, really. Just don't go in any more. Find something else - anything else. If everyone only worked at what they believed in – we would not have all these toxic chemicals polluting our world. There would not be any nuclear waste, because no one would mine the raw material. There would still be fish stocks in the sea because no one would have used driftnets. We would not be losing our sources of oxygen (trees) because people wouldn't cut them down destroying huge amounts of the surrounding land and ecosystems etc.

Many times I hear the argument … "but if I didn't do it, someone else would do it". How about "If we all lived by our principles, no one would do it"? Or even just let someone else do it then.

There are 5 basic moral precepts that we should not break and we should not do any work that breaks them:

- ☐ Do not kill any living thing
- ☐ Do not lie – tell false hoods
- ☐ Do not indulge in sexual misconduct
- ☐ Do not steal anything
- ☐ Do not indulge in intoxicants - else you may be tempted to break the other four precepts

By doing so we harm ourselves, following these precepts is sila, moral conduct. We harm our soul and our psyche when we do not follow sila. If our work involves any of the above, desist at once.

We will feel better for it. These precepts form the basis of buddhism, which is not a religion, it is a way of life.

What instead?

We all have unique talents and gifts. We all have the ability to be creative in some way. If we all pursued our creativity to the full, there would be no time or energy for destruction and wars. We need to find out what our unique talents are. Sit down somewhere quiet for half an hour and work it out. Perhaps we take a train or bus every day? We could use our journey time wisely. Think about what else we could be doing, either on the journey (I wrote the first draft of this book on such a journey!) or with our life in general.

Once we have our list, work out what we enjoy doing that uses those talents.

We are now ready for our career change. How do we turn our enjoyment into a career or job? Firstly find out if others do something similar. See if they need help. Perhaps we should set up our own business? Become self-reliant. Provide our own work. I know it may not be easy. I have trouble with this myself. It takes courage and confidence to start up your own business. Take time, work out how you can get to where you need to be. Persevere. Build on your assets.

We might need a 5-year plan in order to get where we want to be. Perhaps we <u>do</u> need to keep our job for the moment so we can save up enough to start our own business? Be flexible with ourselves. Perhaps we need to study or gain a qualification before we can do what we really want.

There are many creative ways of making money. A friend of mine used to enjoy going to car boot sales and now she makes an extra £200 or so a week through selling all her stuff through the internet. Anyone can do this kind of thing if we get really creative and think about what we really want and like. Then it's just a matter of applying it.

One thing I know for certain if we do not try, we will not succeed.

If we are certain that what we are doing is the right thing; then don't give up. If we are surrounded by people who believe in us; continue. We will be rewarded. It has taken me over 20 years to decide what it is I should be doing with my life and I finally have the answers. It's been easy to decide what I <u>don't</u> want to do with my life. But what I do want? That's been much harder.

I have written this book to offer help and guidance to us all. Use the bits we like – don't worry about the bits we don't like. This book is to inspire us in our own life – to create our own life as we want it.

Most of us are aware of only one life at any time, so we should all make the best of our life when and whilst we can.

The world appears to be speeding up: "time" runs faster and faster, we travel at an ever-faster pace to keep up with ourselves. 200 years ago, most people had not and did not travel outside of their own towns or villages. 50 years ago people began to commute from one town to another on a regular basis. 10 years ago air travel became commonplace for many. 5 years ago public transport and roads became a big issue. Now, many of us are working weird hours so that we can travel without being crushed by the throngs that must get to London or Manhattan or Downtown LA or wherever, before 9am. In the West we have moved from manufacturing industries to service industries. (Though this is also rapidly changing with many companies in the UK relocating their call centres to India, so what will we do then?) If we don't know our way around a computer we are almost unemployable these days.

The great excuses are now "The computers have gone down" or "Well it says so on the computer". The computer has become the new god whom we must all serve. They have their uses, it is true but I am old enough to remember the myths that first came with them. "They will reduce paper use"; "They will make our lives easier"; "We won't lose records anymore"; "There won't be any more mistakes".

I am sure we can all see the irony in these statements!

So think about your life, your job. What would you rather be doing? Then go do it! More and more people are coming to this decision and not regretting it! Be one of them.

<u>Action Points</u>

- Work out what your unique talents are
- Work out what you enjoy doing
- See if there is any way to combine the above into a profession
- Change your job for something you enjoy

<u>Beliefs</u>

The crown chakra is violet and is about spiritual awakening. You become totally aware of your True Self. It represents the pineal gland and the cerebral cortex. Warriors of the Rainbow: your time is now! We need to wake up to ourselves and start affecting the world in the right way, let us bring the mass human consciousness up to the point where we all want to live on our planet, rather than die on her and take everyone and everything else with us!

Many of us try out different belief systems within our lifetime. This is a good thing, as we try to decide what fits best for ourselves. Most of us start off with the belief systems that our families have, of course, but this system is not always right for any individual. Sadly this often causes frictions within the family unit, as parents and other family members become upset that the offspring have decided that a particular belief is not for them. It needs to be understood that the micro follows the macro and we can easily see that although such problems are bad for the individuals concerned, it is not a huge trauma for the world. However if an entire religion or large group of people decide that they are going to be intolerant of other beliefs, then we can have much trauma and trouble in the world. This is the situation we currently seem to be facing.

I have been through a few different belief systems, I was lucky enough not to be brought up in a religious household, my parents were very sure that they wanted to allow my brother and I to make up our own minds about the existence or otherwise of some kind of Supreme Being. I remember very clearly feeling that there was no such thing as God, I was an atheist, I thought that religion was for those who could not handle the fact that there is no point to life, that when you die, that's it. No next life, no going to Heaven, none of this, just oblivion. Over time I found that this belief was very depressing and unjust. I didn't want to believe such things. So over time, different experiences and with study of other systems of belief, I found myself coming to some very different conclusions. I feel now that I have my own belief system, one that works for me. Many of its components share much of the Buddhist belief system, yet it is not Buddhism. I also use some Pagan beliefs too. I have a deep sense of the sacredness of all life and a huge desire to protect all life. I celebrate the solstices and equinoxes of the year, these seem appropriate times to think about our life and how it is going. A time to prepare for Winter, to think about the planting to be done over Spring. I feel that the Earth is my Mother, Gaia, She gave us all life, without Her we would not exist, we would have nowhere to live. As Her children, it is up to each of us to look after Her as best we can, as she looks after us. If we do not, the consequences are dire for the entire human race and all the other species currently living on Her. She provides us with a beautiful planet to live on, with amazing food to eat, with fresh air to breathe, with clean water to drink; yet here we are throwing it all back in Her face and abusing it, stopping certain members of our family from having access to this bounty.

I also believe that there is The Universe, a powerful Loving Energy Force that is also indifferent to us. It loves us, it has compassion for us, it directs our lives and to some extent everything is preordained, though there is always Fate and Destiny which can throw in their twopennyworth at any time. We do have free will, everything that happens to us is a consequence of our actions. There is Karma. If you do wrong to another, something bad will happen to you and most likely in this lifetime, not the next.

With this set of beliefs, I am able to explain to myself why most things happen.

If God/Yahweh/Allah/Buddha/The Universal Life Force/whatever exists, then this superbeing must love us, else it/he/she would not have created us. If it loves us, then it is not vengeful. If it is not vengeful, there is no hell, except that which we create on Earth. If there is no hell, there is nothing to fear.

All that will happen when we die is we return to the loving energy that this Being is. Many of us of a religious persuasion will say that we feel this loving energy in our lives now. It is true. We all do, whether or not we seek to find it, listen to it or accept it. This is why we need to learn to love ourselves first. If we do not believe that we deserve this all-encompassing love, then we will not feel it. How can we? We have told ourselves we do not deserve it, so it will not be found. Or that it does not exist, so it will not be found.

It can be felt in many different ways. It is the individual's choice.

I believe that when we die - and this is something that happens to us all, sooner or later at a time of our choosing, whether we believe this or not - our deeds in this life will be added to the deeds in our past lives and we will see whether the overall balance has been to reduce the love in this world, or to increase the love in this world. If we have sought to increase the love, we will move on up a level, if we have sought only to decrease love, to spread hatred and fear instead, then we will remain at the same level or even drop down. We might be in a position where others will have control over us and hate us. If we feel we are the recipient of negative energy, in whatever form, it may be that we are being paid back for a previous life. Our task is to overcome our natural feelings of hatred to those who seek to make our life a living hell, to send back to them peace, love and forgiveness instead.

This is what Jesus did. Truly he was "The Way". If we follow his teachings with love, we will ascend in the manner He did. I talk of Jesus, yet I do not consider myself a Christian. The current religions that claim to be Christian have been perverted by the powers that be for too long to have much left that is real. Witness if you will the number of wars that have been caused by religion. There is not one True religious leader that would say these are good. All religions should decry war. Any religion that says that war is holy, or necessary in order for the religion to survive, has been perverted by the powers that be.

No one can take our beliefs away from us. No other religion is a threat to any others. We can believe different things without coming into conflict over our beliefs.

It is not necessary for everyone to believe the same thing, in fact all religions say exactly the same thing at their heart:

Love one another

That is all.

If we can be tolerant, if we can project love instead of hate, we can and will save the planet and ourselves. Nothing else will work. This is the lesson we are all here to learn and the sooner we do so, the better for us all.

The Earth is in pain. Surely you can feel it? In the weather, the sudden winds and droughts, floods and waves. Earthquakes where previously there was calm. This is the Earth's way of telling us that She is hurting. This is why we must all send her love. What happens to a child that is unloved? It is more likely to become a being of hatred who lies, steals, cheats, kills. Think what might happen to a planet that is unloved? The same thing and we are witnessing the results now. The more of us that tell her we love Her and act with love towards her, the better She will become. The planet is made up of energy, just as we are. She is no different.

The powers that be do not want us to become aware. They do not want us to start to love. They wrongly believe they will lose their power if everyone is aware how much power each of us has. Please do not think I am suggesting that I or anyone else is superior here. I am not. I am human, as are you. We need to send the powers that be love too. They are most sorely in need of it.

No one has the right to dictate to us how we should live, but our own conscience should dictate to us that we should not live at the expense of others. There is no need to. As I said before, we can all be fed, clothed, sheltered, educated and cared for, for the price of four weeks worth of arms sales.

Of course, the powers that be would have you think it is not that simple.

YES IT IS!

Demand it of our politicians.

Demand that the International Monetary Fund writes off the debt "owed" by certain countries. Their debts have been repaid many times over already.

Change our beliefs and we change the world. The more people that believe that change can happen, that peace will prevail, the more likely it is to occur.

One thing is for sure, it won't occur whilst we believe it to be impossible.

We all have a part to play in the future of this planet and of humanity.

There are Guardian Angels ready to help us, all we need do is ask for the help and it shall be given. "Ask and you shall receive," said Jesus. This was what He was referring to, not to great material treasures, which leave us empty and wanting more.

We will never have enough if we pursue this line. Nothing will ever be enough. We could have all the wealth available on the planet and still we would want more and we would be scared of losing it.

We have only to look at the lives of the rich and famous to see the truth of this.

Fate has its part to play, as does God/Allah/Yahweh/whatever. It exists. It exists to help us, if we ever ask.

We need to do what we can in our own life to live outside the powers that be.

Take control of your life again.

Live free.

Live in peace and harmony.

It is possible, just do it.

All I am saying is do not accept everything that we are told. There are many advantages for governments to keep people in the dark about what is really going on. Find out for yourself. Even some scientists will lie and cheat to get their theories to be accepted. Those that do not conform to the preconceived order will find themselves discredited in the most vile ways. We must not believe everything we see or hear. The media is following government or corporate orders to a greater or lesser degree. Who decides what is news? Who decides what is a story worth printing and what will never see the light of day?

At a personal level we may have noticed that the people who get a certain job are not necessarily those best able to do it. Jobs often go to those who agree with the management. Those who will bow down before them. Those who will carry out orders. This is fine in the army, but may not be so useful in the agencies that look after people. If you are unfortunate enough to have needed the help of social services, you have no doubt come up against people who try to make things as difficult for you as possible. They are just doing their job, which is to save the government money. In spite of all the rhetoric about what they should do, their actual purpose is to ensure that the government does not pay out money. They need to keep it all for giving themselves huge pay rises and for arming the world, instead of helping it. There are also those who work in Social Services who are genuinely wanting to help people out, but they will not receive promotion, they will not be "recognised" for their work within their department.

If you do not believe me, investigate for yourself. If you do so with an open mind, you will find what I am saying is true.

Why have we just had a war with (inset name of last war)? To focus your attention in the wrong place, to keep you so busy worrying about imagined terrorist threats, that you do not have time or energy to devote to thinking about how to improve the world. Now we have a new threat... Covid! I am not saying it does not exist, it truly does, but the actual harm it can do has been ramped up out of proportion and the world is currently living in fear from it.

Look within your heart and the answer is there. Can't find anything? Go on a meditation course. Allow yourself the time and space to see things differently. I know it is hard, if not almost impossible for most people in Western society to do this. It is kept this way purposely. Keep us hard at work all day, every day. Not allowed to think for ourselves. Keep drinking the alcohol, it will surely rot our brain, just as each sip kills more brain cells which are not replaced. Become more stupid. This is what the powers that be want. More willing robots to work hard doing those jobs that have to be done for the good of all.

This currently is the purpose of school. To brainwash our children into the belief that this is all there is and we just have to get on with it. Find a job and choose our partner, get a house, have kids, perpetuate the whole cycle over again. Never move out of our beliefs, do not question the nature of our orders. Cut ourselves off from other people, only know people from work, spend more time with them than with your loved ones.

And so it goes.

Ensure you build up enemies, people you have never met, or have any understanding of, yet we are told they are our enemies.

I have not come to these ideas through other entities outside of myself. It is all just from being a person who does not fit in with the status quo. I don't just accept what I am told. I do the research myself. I find out for myself. Do the same. There are loads of websites in the back of this book, go check some of them out.

Do not believe that we elected our government. Look at the US. The second Bush was bought in. Most people did not vote for him. It is the same story all over the world. Democracy does not really exist. It is a fabrication designed to fool us into thinking we have some control over our lives. It is the only thing we have right now, so we must still use it for now. Vote like your future depends on it!

There have been artificial barriers set up against others. Really we are all the same. All humans want the same things. Just because we speak different languages, live in different parts of the world, have different beliefs none of this makes us less human. If anything, it makes us more human.

We need to learn tolerance and acceptance. Yes, it is hard but there are many examples of fine human beings who have forgiven those who have hurt them or their loved ones. We need to come out of our ignorance, come out of our misery. Learn to love all, or at least to tolerate all. It can be done in our current lifetime.

Keep positive. There are good things happening all the time. Our media is now an instrument of the powers that be, set up to keep us down, to make us think there is no hope, so that the only thing we can do is to keep hiding in our own minds and worlds and not worry about the state of the world. Who decides what is newsworthy? Who decides what makes a story? Why is there no positive news? Why do the papers focus so much on crime and drug abuse when crime rates in the UK have dropped dramatically over the last few years? They want to keep us scared. Keep us from wanting to go outside, make us think that the only way we can be safe is to have ourselves stamped and encoded in the government systems. How long before we all have microchips embedded in our ears or bar codes on the backs of our necks?

The World is our world, our planet too. If we can all take responsibility for our planet, if we can all think of this planet as ours, belonging to us all, it would make all the difference to how we look after it. We would, in fact, look after it.

How do we do that? Simply by starting to look after the part that we live in. Imagine if we just started to collect the litter in our local park or riverside walk, just because it was there? What if we just started to remove rubbish from the streets near our house on our way to or from anywhere? Believe you can make a difference and you can.

Everything is all just ever-changing patterns of energy and our purpose is to evolve spiritually until we realise this on an experiential level, only then will we be able to live in peace and harmony with other Beings.

<u>Action Points</u>

- Examine our beliefs; do they make us happy?
- Question the nature of our orders
- Do not just accept things the way they are
- If you can't change the world, change yourself; and if you can't change yourself, then change your world – Matt Johnson
- Never for one moment doubt that a small band of individuals can change the world, indeed it is the only thing which ever has – Margaret Mead

<u>**Solutions**</u>

Take the blinkers from your eyes

The powers that be in this world, the governments and so-called elected representatives have been forcing their version of the truth and perception on us for long enough. It is time to remove the blinkers and see for ourselves. This means realising that capitalism is not the answer and is not sustainable, never could be. Materialism is what we have been sold in order to deflect us from the Truth of who we really are. There are alternative futures, ones in which we respect our planet.

There have been many whom have tried to tell us the Truth, all the great religious leaders, for a start. **In every case**, the powers that be have perverted this message, rearranged the words, cut out the bits that would set us free from the fear of death, that would allow us to realise that everything is all just energy and as such, what we do to others, we truly do to ourselves.

It is now time for everyone to realise the way of things. Plato said that there would always be a small number of people able to think for themselves and judge the Truth, but now we need a larger number to come to this realisation. We do not have to follow orders. We do have free will. If we use it wisely then we will have a planet fit for our children to inherit.

Do not underestimate the Power of Positive Thought. As part of our daily exercise routine, we need to ensure we spend some time sending healing energy to the Earth. She really needs it now, from as many people as possible. My cousin was involved in a coach accident that killed his best friend sitting next to him and he himself was injured as badly as possible without dying. He had severe head injuries and was in a coma for some time. I sent him reiki from New Zealand, where I was at the time, I know that many others were praying for him and adding him to their thoughts. He has now recovered so well that the doctors are amazed. He is almost normal, just has problems finding the right words sometimes. The only explanation I can offer for his extremely good recovery is the power of positive thought sent out by so many people. It healed my cousin, just think how well we could heal ourselves and our planet, if we all put our minds to it!

We are living in the most exciting times, The End Times as many religions have called it. It is not really the End, merely a new beginning. A time for us all to start thinking with our hearts instead of our greed. It is possible. We all start off with the purest hearts and minds, which gradually become deluded by our life and experiences on the Planet. The test is to see through this, to continue to love against all the odds. It does us no good to hate the powers that be, we must instead do as Ghandi suggested and offer back love. Without love we are powerless.

Yes, love conquers all. It will always do so.

Material gain is worthless. Surely the evidence of this is obvious for all to see. Look around you, read the tabloids; are the rich and famous happy? The only ones who are, are those who have a highly spiritual outlook. Those who seek gain for the sake of gain are miserable beyond all measure, hence their show of fear and hatred of all they do not understand.

There are positive examples that we are changing and that the world is coming to these realisations; the huge anti-war movement that preceded the Gulf Wars this time around. So many people coming together to say that war is wrong. There was no justification. To go to war for economic gain is the essence of evil as it manifests in our plane. There is no justification for war. There are no winners, only losers. Even the companies that win the contracts to rebuild don't really win.

Once again the powers that be have perverted money to their own coffers and damn everyone else.

We can keep technology, but we must ensure it is actually useful and does no harm to our planet. It is the only one we have.

We have all the solutions to the environmental problems that befall our Planet.

We can solve it all now. The powers that be choose not to do so, in order for them to continue to make lots of money, even though it is not making them happy, only serving to build up fear in themselves. Fear of losing their great treasures while people on the planet starve.

If all the governments of the world agreed to stop spending money on weapons of mass destruction for a mere 4 weeks, every single person on this planet could be fed, clothed, watered, housed, educated and treated for an entire year. If we need more reason to be annoyed with the arms trade, perhaps we need to remember that whenever a country does not pay for its arms, as many smaller countries do not, then it is the tax payer who pays the deficit. Yes, that's right, if someone defaults on an arms payment: we pay for it with our taxes. That is why our hospitals are in such dire need and we do not have enough money to pay our teachers properly.

Why does this not happen? Fear and greed. These are our only barriers to becoming fully conscious beings. If we can all agree to banish fear and greed from our own lives, then it will spread like wildfire across the world.

The pyramid structure of hierarchy is wrong, it is not those at the top who have the power, as they would have us believe, but the masses at the bottom. If we want to survive, to give our children the love and planet they deserve, then believe what I have written and make use of it in your own life.

If we change, we will affect other people and they too will change by chain reactions and ripple effect and so it will go on, until the powers that be have no choice but to change.

Believe we are powerful and have control over our life. You are the only person who has control over your life. Use it wisely.

We have all the solutions to the world's problems. They are just not being implemented.

If everyone had a few solar panels on their roof, if everyone had a small wind turbine, we would reduce our dependence on fossil fuels and nuclear power for electricity. If we turned off the TV, computer and stereo every night, instead of leaving it all on standby, we'd save 5% of our current electricity use. If street lamps ran on solar power, if shops and offices didn't leave lights on all night, we'd reduce our power needs dramatically. If we used our central heating only when necessary, didn't heat up our hot water boilers all the time, but only when we needed them. There are so many ways to cut down on electricity use. So many people in the world using it and that number increasing daily as India and China try to catch up with Western standards. The emerging new economic powers need to have the state of the art technology, not our old cast-offs. Tesla had a system of free energy that he was working on, but guess what? The powers that be didn't like that idea and discredited him and ensured that he took his knowledge and his work to the grave.

We need to rid ourselves of the idea that making money is all that counts.

Economic gain is all there is. If we do not, we will not have a planet to live on.

Currently the law states that a company must ensure that the shareholders get the highest profits possible. All other considerations are secondary to this. The law says that a company must pollute if it cheaper than not polluting, because the profits of the shareholders must come first. This is a ridiculous state of affairs. What chance does the planet have with laws like these? What chance do workers have with such laws? Such laws need to be repealed, they need to change. We have the power to ask our government representatives to change these laws. If we do not even try to change it, we will never know. If many of us ask, they will have to take notice. This is always the way. We have the power to not vote them in next time.

If all the empty housing was turned into hostels for the homeless who could earn a place in them by litter picking and community gardening, we would not only solve housing shortages, but get people off the streets, off the drugs and beginning to have some self-esteem back again. Not to mention the fact that we'd all be living in a more pleasant environment as there would be no litter and there would be well-kept gardens and green spaces in all our towns and cities.

If more people began to meditate, to see that the only way to gain true happiness was to find it inside themselves, not through the buying of material items, by having power over others, by abusing themselves or others, we could have a society of joy. Where the young are not committing suicide daily as they cannot cope with life anymore.

Can you see it? Can you envision another world? Where we all live in harmony with each other? The more of us who hold a positive vision, who believe that change is possible and desirable, the more likely it is to happen. If we do not believe it is possible, then it will never happen. However, slowly, slowly, more and more people are coming to the decision that they want a more peaceful life, one where they don't have to spend hours in rush hour traffic, queues or crowded public transport. A life where they have time to be creative, time to be with their loved ones, Time to spend in proper leisure, not just the 2 week family holiday in Majorca. A society where the good side of humanity comes to the fore.

Why is there so much crime? Perhaps there's not really. Where do we get our facts from? The media? We have to understand that the media are controlled by the powers that be. They say only what they want us to know about. They want us to remain in fear. Stay at home, go to work, be good and we can have our 2 weeks holiday in Majorca. That's the message they want us to have. They also want us to buy their newspaper, watch their TV station, listen to their radio waves. Again, we have the power to not do that. Find a more enjoyable way to spend time.

If crime figures in the UK have been falling by 30% over the past 2 years, why are there ever more stories about crime in the media? In order to keep us under control. That's why.

Yet most people are scared of change. Would rather stay in an uncomfortable, yet familiar situation, than break out of it and try something new. Dare to be different. Think for yourself. Don't believe what religions tell you, believe what your heart tells you. Your heart may well be in line with a religious dogma and if you really feel it saying something to you: good. Go with it. But if it feels at all wrong for you; then don't. Stop and think about the alternatives instead. How do we want our life to be? Do we want to be in control of it, or do we want to give our life up to someone else? Some other power?

There is help out there for people who are being abused, whether you are an adult or a child. We just need to find the courage to do it. Make the changes that are necessary for our emotional survival. Tell someone. Speak out. There are phone numbers, there are counsellors, there are those in authority who would help.

Waging war depends on having young, strong men and women who are patriotic enough to kill because their government tells them to. They are brave young people who believe they are doing the right thing. Often in many countries, the army is made up of conscripted people. They do not have the choice, except to go to jail if they refuse. In Israel, your job in civilian society depends on what you did in the army, so you do not have much choice. Yet there is always choice. It might not be a good one, but choice is there nonetheless. You can claim to be insane, that will get you out of active service. You will have a hard time getting work, but at least you will not have blood on your hands. Many young Israelis are not happy with being forced to track down and kill or imprison Palestinians, it is not the young who have a quarrel with the Palestinians, it is the old and these are not the ones who are fighting. If every person only did what they wanted to do, instead of what they felt forced to do, there would not be so much bloodshed on our planet.

Huge increases in terrorism... are there? It is being readily reported by our media every day; the media determined to get us scared, scared of asylum seekers, scared of jobs being taken by others, scared of being attacked on the streets, scared of having our homes robbed: fear, fear, fear. This is what the media portrays and breeds. It is not there to inform us. What are the stories in the papers? Some rich person being upset, some film star getting divorced, some model spilling the beans on her affair with a married football manager, some media "star" being seen in the right places, crime, crime, crime, death and war, economic forces... is any of it relevant to our life? Probably not. We could live quite happily without being aware of any of it. I am tempted to say we would live much happier without the knowledge of any of it. It is just other people's negatives thoughts thrown down onto paper or beamed out through radio waves to your radio or television set. Do we need anyone else's negative thoughts in our life? Try having a couple of weeks off from reading papers or listening to or watching the news. See if you feel happier for it.

Imagine if the media were full of positive images of people instead? Imagine if we were informed of the good projects that are happening around the world? What if there was positive music being beamed out from our music channels?

Why do people take drugs? To a certain extent, it has always been so, but these for ceremonies and important occasions. These days it is from boredom, or to shut out the harsh realities of a shitty life, to stop us from thinking about hurts, either that we caused to another or someone caused to us. To escape reality. Yet reality is all there is, so what's the point in trying to escape from it? If we don't like our reality it is better to try and do something about it to change it, rather than just do drugs and pretend it isn't happening! For many trapped in the poverty cycle it can seem the only glimmer of hope. Sell drugs, maybe we'll make enough to get out of the tower blocks; except that we never do. Just spend it on a bigger TV, the latest Playstation, new car, whatever, it doesn't really add to our quality of life. Altered states of consciousness are worth pursuing, but to learn from them, not to try and remain in that state forever. There is much magic that can be done with altered states.

How can we solve the crises of hospital waiting lists? By not creating them in the first place. By asking people to be responsible for their own health. We know if we smoke that we have a much bigger chance of lung cancer, throat cancer, heart disease, and general poor health in later life, so why do it? Why give our money to the legal drug barons? Stop it now. There are many ways of stopping, many avenues of help to seek. Is it cool to have lung cancer? Do we look sexier with a hole in our throat? These are questions worth asking of ourselves.

Many cancers are caused by poor lifestyle choices. Poor diet is paramount. Good, fresh, organic fruit and vegetables is what everyone needs more of. Eating conventional produce only builds up the toxins in our system, all those organo-phosphates, which are not removed by washing the fruit or veg, else every time it rained the farmers would be reapplying the agro-chemicals, which they do not. Sure, some diseases are genetic and there may be little we can do to stop it. There will always be a certain amount of ill-health. It is only natural. We still have to die. We have to die of something. Not everyone who is born is destined to live until they are 120 years old! All I'm saying is that there is much that can be done for ourselves by ourselves to help ensure that we are not a statistic, waiting in vain for a hospital appointment. If you are able to afford private care, that seems like a good alternative, allow the national health service to be best utilised by those who cannot afford private care. We should still be seeking to help those who cannot help themselves. Can we get the balance right? Look after ourselves as much as possible, yet still be prepared to help those who cannot do so?

Alcohol is another huge cause of ill-health. Too many people drink too much and they know it, but don't seem willing or able to stop. Why? Most people who drink too much do so because they are unhappy for whatever reason. They may not even admit their own unhappiness to themselves, but nevertheless this is the cause. If this sounds like you: Perhaps it is time to get wise with yourself. Look at yourself. Seek help, go to counselling or enrol in a counselling course. You will increase your self-awareness and help yourself come to terms with whatever it is you are unhappy with. Maybe it's your marriage, maybe it's your childhood. Many, many reasons, but you need to find out what it is. Why do you drink so much? For those of us who don't, it's very hard to watch a loved one slowly drinking themselves to death. We are helpless. It is down to the drinker to stop. They are the only who can. Maybe you think it's your only pleasure in Life? Time to get a new Life! Whatever it takes.

Just Do It!

<u>**Appendix 1**</u>

There are several versions of a Prophecy from the Native American Indians which describe a near destruction of Life on Earth and how Earth is returned to the Paradise Garden of Eden it once was. The longest and most detailed prophecy I have come across is that told to Lelanie Fuller Stone by her grandmother.

There was an old lady, from the "Cree" tribe, named "Eyes of Fire", who prophesied that one day, because of the white mans' or Yo-ne-gis' greed, there would come a time, when the fish would die in the streams, the birds would fall from the air, the waters would be blackened, and the trees would no longer be, mankind as we would know it, would all but cease to exist. There would come a time when the "keepers of the legend, stories, culture rituals, and myths, and all the Ancient Tribal Customs" would be needed to restore us to health.

They would be mankind's' key to survival, they were the "Warriors of the Rainbow".

There would come a day of awakening when all the peoples of all the tribes would form a New World of Justice, Peace, Freedom and recognition of the Great Spirit. The "Warriors of the Rainbow" would spread these messages and teach all peoples of the Earth or "Elohi". They would teach them how to live the "Way of the Great Spirit". They would tell them of how the world today has turned away from the Great Spirit and that is why our Earth is "Sick". The "Warriors of the Rainbow" would show the peoples that this "Ancient Being" (the Great Spirit), is full of love and understanding, and teach them how to make the "Earth or Elohi" beautiful again. These Warriors would give the people principles or rules to follow to make their path right with the world. These principles would be those of the Ancient Tribes. The Warriors of the Rainbow would teach the people of the ancient practices of Unity, Love and Understanding. They would teach of Harmony among people in all four comers of the Earth. Like the Ancient Tribes, they would teach the people how to pray to the Great Spirit with love that flows like the beautiful mountain stream, and flows along the path to the ocean of life. Once again, they would be able to feel joy in solitude and in councils. They would be free of petty jealousies and love all mankind as their brothers, regardless of colour, race or religion. They would feel happiness enter their hearts, and become as one with the entire human race. Their hearts would be pure and radiate warmth, understanding and respect for all mankind, Nature, and the Great Spirit. They would once again fill their minds, hearts, souls, and deeds with the purest of thoughts. They would seek the beauty of the Master of Life - the Great Spirit! They would find strength and beauty in prayer and the solitudes of life. Their children would once again be able to run free and enjoy the treasures of Nature and Mother Earth. Free from the fears of toxins and destruction, wrought by the Yo-ne-gi and his practices of greed.

The rivers would again run clear, the forests be abundant and beautiful, the animals and birds would be replenished. The powers of the plants and animals would again be respected and conservation of all that is beautiful would become a way of life. The poor, sick and needy would be cared for by their brothers and sisters of the Earth. These practices would again become a part of their daily lives. The leaders of the people would be chosen in the old way - not by their political party, or who could speak the loudest, boast the most, or by name calling or mud slinging, but by those whose actions spoke the loudest. Those who demonstrated their love, wisdom, and courage and those who showed that they could and did work for the good of all, would be chosen as the leaders or Chiefs. They would be chosen by their "quality" and not the amount of money they had obtained. Like the thoughtful and devoted "Ancient Chiefs", they would understand the people with love, and see that their young were educated with the love and wisdom of their surroundings. They would show them that miracles can be accomplished to heal this world of its ills, and restore it to health and beauty.

The tasks of these "Warriors of the Rainbow" are many and great. There will be terrifying mountains of ignorance to conquer and they shall find prejudice and hatred. They must be dedicated, unwavering in their strength, and strong of heart. They will find willing hearts and minds that will follow them on this road of returning "Mother Earth" to beauty and plenty - once more. The day will come; it is not far away. The day that we shall see how we owe our very existence to the people of all tribes that have maintained their culture and heritage. Those that have kept the rituals, stories, legends, and myths alive. It will be with this knowledge, the knowledge that they have preserved, that we shall once again return to "harmony" with Nature, Mother Earth, and mankind. It will be with this knowledge that we shall find our "Key to our Survival".

There is a shorter version of this Prophecy that also comes from a Native Tribe, this time the Hopi:

When the Earth is dying there shall arise a new tribe of all colours and all creeds. This tribe shall be called the Warriors of the Rainbow and it will put its faith in actions not words.

Another older prophecy says:

There will come a time when the Earth is sick and the animals and plants begin to die, Then the Indians will regain their spirit and gather people of all nations, colours and beliefs to join together in the fight to save the Earth: The Rainbow Warriors.

I find it interesting that these prophecies all emerge from the same continent, from the country that is doing its utmost to destroy our Planet; The USA. I think many of us often feel overwhelmed by the destruction we see going on around us. What can we do in the face of such evil? And yet, these people who would destroy us are not evil. Sadly they truly believe that the destruction they are causing will make the World a better place. The US government truly believes that when the entire world can buy McDonald's and Coke then we will all be happy. Happy meals, happy people, you see! This in spite of the overwhelming evidence against this being so. The US has the highest crime rate per capita in the World, yet seems unable to link this with its utter belief in Capitalism as the ideal paradigm.

Appendix 2

Grandmother Circle Ceremony

The Grandmothers

There are eight Grandmothers who are represented by stones placed at the eight compass points. The Grandmothers are our ancestors. They are the ancestors of every human, as all humans originally came from one place. These Grandmothers then have access to much knowledge and are able to guide any of us who ask with reverence and right mind.

In the **North** sits **Grandmother Star Nation**; she understands the soul purpose, ancestry, she is global energy. It is all so big, we have very little idea of how the Universe was created, how it is saved, but the people of Star Nation, they helped with all that. They carry the oldest wisdom, what they know is scientifically beyond us, they are a wonderful people. There was a time when we did not eat, nothing ate anything, it was a wonderful time. If you wish to visit Star Nation, you can at any time stand on the ground and pray to catch a ray of Star Light, it is faint, but there; the Light will come to you and carry you up to Star Nations. You can be carried off to other Worlds. You don't even want to eat, you are free. Breathing is nourishment

To the **South** we have **Grandmother Moon** whose child-like qualities teach us about the inner child and renewal. Hers is a waxing and waning energy, she is intuition, cycles, water and feelings, she is very gentle and protects the young ones. Enlightenment of the moon.

In the **East** of course, we have **Grandmother Sun**; she has a creative strength, she illuminates problems, she is about initiation, her energy is creative bursts, she is about new growth, new shoots. The warmth of the sun, the Hopi get up before sunrise as they believe it is rude to the sun to still be in bed when it comes up.

Opposite, in the **West** we find **Grandmother Earth** who is so nurturing to us all, she is about the physical body, nurturing seeds, especially creative seeds, hers is a grounding energy, she is the seasons: during the winter the bears seek hibernation and in the spring after the long rest, the animals are ready to work. The mother bear comes out of her cave very proud with her cubs behind.

The **South-West** is where **Grandmother Shaman** lives; she can be difficult for us to understand, she deals with the ethereal, her place is the Journey, she is the mind and soul healer she is about understanding oneself

To the **South-East** sits **Grandmother Midwife**; she helps with the birthing of projects, childcare, childbirth

In the **North-West** is **Grandmother Death** who helps us to let go, to deal with endings and changes. Ending things in the right way, being free to move on. Death and Mid-wife come together, Death teaches us all to let go what we don't need anymore, to be able to make a change

Finally in the **North-East** we have **Grandmother Priestess**; she is our medicine woman, she knows the animal totems and she can help with physical healing

Purification

All who wish to take part in the ceremony must first be purified with the smoke from the sage bush. This process is known as smudging. White sage is placed in a clay goblet and set fire to. The flames are fanned out with a collection of feathers. The smoke is strong and purifying, the smoke is fanned over the body, front and back starting at the feet and working the way up to the head. One person smudges everyone who arrives for the ceremony, this person is also smudged. Start at the feet and work your way up the body, the person turns round and you do their back. After they turn to face you again and you place the feather on their forehead and say "All your relations". This reminds us that we are about to visit our ancestors, who are the relations of everyone.

The Tools

A sacred cloth is placed on the floor with the corners pointing out the major compass directions. The eight Grandmothers are taken from their bag and placed at each of the eight compass points; a white candle is placed in the centre of the cloth and lit.

One person volunteers to drum for the Journey. The drum looks like the Celtic bodhran, with its circle of wood forming the band round which the buffalo skin is stretched. There is some knotted rope on the backside of the bodhran for the player to hold. In this case a stick with a large padded beater is used rather than the small double-ended stick that is used in Celtic Folk music. The drum beats slowly, heartbeat-like to create a timelessness about the experience, though in truth the time is set at 15 or 20 minutes.

There is a cushion for each person to sit on.

The Ceremony

The Ceremony begins with each person choosing which Grandmother they wish to speak to, ideally they should sit in front of her. It is best if each Grandmother has a visitor and that one visits each in turn. A chakra meditation is first read out to allow everyone to open their chakras fully and reach a higher plane of energy than that which they usually inhabit. In this Higher State of Consciousness it is possible to connect with the Universe and find the Grandmothers. The drum beats throughout the whole ceremony. After the meditation the Journey begins.

During this time you seek the Grandmother, you must first work out where you are, so you look around. You must ask your question. You must be very clear or you will not get a clear answer. Start by asking for her "Where is Grandmother XXX?" Look around you. What do you see? What do you feel? What creatures can you see? What plants are there? If you see a creature ask it "Where is Grandmother XXX?" Everywhere you go, keep asking "Where is Grandmother XXX?" If you see an animal, follow it, it may lead you to her, keep asking and searching; whatever you see is there for you. Go down into things, perhaps a cave, or the roots of a tree, the Grandmother will come to you if you keep searching. Do not worry about whether you are making up the things that come into your mind. It does not matter; the vision is what the vision is. Accept it for what it is and do not worry about where it comes from. When you find the Grandmother you must be very polite to the Elder and you ask her your question, listen carefully to what she tells you. Sometimes the answer is a bit strange and you cannot understand it. That is why you should have a diary and you can write it down and when you go home and sleep, you may see the Journey again in your mind and things may become clear. When you have your reply, thank her and give her a present. If you have nothing in your pockets, then look around for a lovely flower or a beautiful stone. You want to give her a present. Ask her for a message to take back to the group.

This message is shared with the group and recorded in the Grandmother Book. After all messages have been passed on and the vision ends, each person may sit for a while and take time to write down what has occurred before they lose it. When each has finished, the person to the left of the drummer starts to tell the Circle of her Journey. She may keep it to just the message for the group if she wishes. After each has told her story, all the rest say "HO!" there is some silent reflection and then we all stand up and join hands. Sometimes a song is sung. The candle is blown out and we record our messages in the Grandmother Book and then leave.

You must visit each Grandmother in turn. The Grandmothers are a Council, they get offended if one person visits only with one Grandmother all the time. They wonder about these people who come only to visit Shaman. You must try to visit each Grandmother, so it will take 8 months to visit and meet each Grandmother.

Grandmother Death – a Journey

It is dark all around. I'm in a forest, walking through. It is very dark, the sky is night overhead and the leaves are very close together… I come to a door in a tree trunk. I go through the door and down a tunnel. It is a long tunnel, filled with roots lining it. Glow worms light the tunnel. I take one as a present for Death.

Eventually I meet a squirrel who shows me into Death's chamber. She is beautiful, young with jet black hair.

I tell her about D (my ex-) – she advises me to cut in half the photo I found and then burn it. Maybe I need to find and burn all photos of him.

Then I see E – she smiles at me. It is good to see her, standing next to Death. It makes me cry. I feel so sad that I cannot speak to her in this world. She smiles at me and gives me a hug.

I give Grandmother Death the glow worm and ask her for a message for the group.

"It is easy to let go;

It is the holding on that causes pain"

Then I thanked her and came back out of the tunnel and arrived very quickly back here.

www.ingramcontent.com/pod-product-compliance
Lightning Source LLC
Chambersburg PA
CBHW031212160726
47992CB00006B/2692